THAT'S LIFE,
It Starts With You!

The Complete Guide How to Overcome Your Daily Excuses.

Liewe Lynette

Baie dankie vir al jou vriendelikheid.
Glo in jouself, wees wie jy wil wees,
lag elke dag dat jou maag pyn.
Leef elke dag asof dit Vrydag is.
Stay great!

Baie liefde

S E R I J K E   G R O B L E R

ISBN: 978-1-4834-5592-1 (sc)
ISBN: 978-1-4834-5591-4 (e)

Lulu Publishing Services rev. date: 08/25/2016

Contents

Dedication

I would in the first place like to dedicate *That's Life, it Starts with You* to my grandmother, Ann Goosen, my parents and my family. My grandmother was a true inspiration to me and I wanted to complete my book in time for her to read it. Sadly, that was not to be as she passed away in September 2013. I miss her and I know that she would really have understood what I was trying to say about making choices about life in this book.

I also dedicate the book to my friends and to all the people who still have a huge influence on my life. Finally, I want to dedicate it to my life partner, Huibre Bouwer, and our son. Huibre has supported me and assisted me to complete my book. She is a true motivator and I love her.

Acknowledgements

I want to acknowledge the Wellness industry, for allowing me to write my story. The company has played a significant role in developing my leadership skills and gave me the opportunity to grow as a person. Through the Gym I received support and guidance from the best leaders in the health and wellness industry.

To JG, thank you for making time in your busy schedule to pre-read some of the chapters and for your honest feedback and guidance.

Heartfelt thanks Les Aupiais for being my writing mentor. You helped me when I had no idea what I was doing.

I also want to thank Monique Goldblatt, who was part of my life when I started writing. You believed in me from day one. Your editing and support assisted in the improvement in my English vocabulary.

Every single person who has had an influence on my life is also acknowledged; this includes everyone who is part of my life and who encouraged me to write my story.

Foreword

Serijke is a South African-born citizen. Although her home language is 'Afrikaans' she has written her book in English, which was very challenging for her and took her three years to complete.

At the age of 11, she was diagnosed with muscular dystrophy. This is an incurable chronic disease that leads to muscle degeneration. Eventually the disease will result in paralysis.

Serijke has many years' experience as General Manager in the health and wellness industry. In this role she not only develops her employees to become the best that they can be but also functions as a mentor and leadership development coach to them. In addition, she is also a motivational and inspirational speaker. As an entrepreneur, Serijke has experience in cattle farming, which she got involved in because of a passion for farming. In 2004 she completed her degree in Human Movement Science. She is a qualified Personal Trainer and recently finished her diploma in Results Coaching. In her spare time, she is a professional life and business coach. She is also an avid entrepreneur business owner.

Her unique personality, self-motivation and determination to succeed has helped her achieve exceptional results in life and professionally. Although her disability has made life challenging, she believes it has driven her to become a go-getter.

Serijke is family-oriented and loves her family, her support structure. She is like a chameleon; as her life or the universe changes, she adjusts quickly and is always looking for solutions to improve things. With her guts and never-give-up attitude, she has coached and helped develop many new leaders.

In this autobiography Serijke shares her life experiences, the lessons she has learnt and how she handled every situation she encountered. With her great values she gives her views and input on, 'The bigger the rock in your road, the harder you need to work to push it out of the way. Don't become your excuses, be the solution.'

Her philosophy in life is, 'I'm more than I appear to be, all the world's power and strength rests in me. I believe that every day in every way, I become better and better.'

Serijke believes in the power of the mind and how it controls and defines who you become. A strong believer that anything is possible if you put your mind to it, she spends time studying the behaviour of people in different scenarios. She does research on the brain and most of her life stories are about how she used her brain to survive her situation.

Chapter One

Funny Walk

My first thought when I began writing this book was that the concept was a bit of a cliché. *Everyone* who has some sort of illness or disability writes a book, don't they? Books written about people who have survived their illness or accident seem to indicate that you have to go through life's challenges to overcome your biggest fears.

Everyone has fears in life, whether they have an illness to deal with or not. The smallest things can make us withdraw from life. We creep into a deep self-aware darkness that makes us want to hide from the world. 'We want to be accepted, we want to fit in. Every day we go out onto the battlefield called life.' (Serijke)

My grandmother consistently amazed me with her strength and willingness to learn new things. She was an expert knitter and cook and always experimented with new recipes and patterns. When I told her that I wanted to write a book, her first reaction was amazement. She had always wanted to write a book but at the age of 91 she couldn't write anymore and had no idea how to work with a computer or to type. She got this twinkle in her eyes when she realised I was taking the opportunity to write early in my life. She told me that every person has a story to tell and that many people will relate to their stories. 'As humans we are just too lazy to share our stories,' she said. My grandmother celebrated 91 birthdays and said every birthday was different. When I asked her what she would like for her 92nd birthday, she replied, 'Anything - as long as it can fit into my room in the old-age home, I'll be happy.' She was long past wanting material things. As she aged, a small gesture or a thoughtful gift meant so much more to her.

I was 11 years old when I was diagnosed with Charcot-Marie-Tooth[1] Disease and I can still remember it as if it was yesterday. Just remembering brings back painful, confusing thoughts and emotions. I had no idea that this was to be part of my life plan.

My parents came to me one day and told me that they had made an appointment for me to see a doctor in The city. This was because they thought it was necessary to investigate the reason why I could not walk on my heels.

The fact that I couldn't walk on my heels did not bother *me* at all and I wondered why it was becoming a big issue. I thought, 'If they really want me to walk on my heels I will exercise so that I'll be able to do so.' I would do anything to help my parents not have sleepless nights worrying about me.

But clearly, the fact that I couldn't walk on my heels was not the point. The first doctor's appointment was a huge mistake. It was a start but we almost made the wrong decision as he did not know what was wrong with me. As a result, he suggested that we cut my Achilles tendons and tighten the tendons so that I would be able to walk on my heels. Fortunately, my parents felt this did not make sense and refused. I thought that I would have looked like a robot walking with tightened tendons.

We went for a second opinion and this time I underwent numerous tests. I remember the day I had to go for a CAT scan well. My mom prepared me for the drum beforehand but little did we know that I was afraid of going into tunnels. We quickly discovered that I was claustrophobic.

I was told to get dressed in a white gown and very uncomfortable underwear. I then lay down on the flat bed part of the CAT scan machine. They pulled a 'thing' over my head.

'Do not move', the radiographer said. 'The only thing you may do when you go into the tunnel, is to breathe. If you feel uncomfortable, you can press this button.'

I felt her put something into my hand.

'Are you ready?'

'I don't think I'll ever be ready for this', I thought. But in a timid voice I replied, 'Yes.'

The tunnel came closer and closer, my breathing became faster and faster. As I entered the tunnel I felt the air growing colder. My thoughts were racing; 'I cannot breathe, there is not enough oxygen in this tunnel. There must be something wrong. I don't want to die in a tunnel, I still have my whole life to live.' Without even realising what I was doing, I pushed the panic button.t. They pulled me out.

'What's wrong my girl?' said my mom, standing right next to me.

'There is no oxygen in that tunnel, Mommy!'

It took my mother 10 minutes to explain that there was enough oxygen in the tunnel; I just needed to go to my 'happy place'.

'Happy place? Do I have a happy place?'

'Where do you feel safe and happy?' she asked

I really had to think about this 'happy place'. On the farm, in my bedroom with my doggy or in the field with my dad in winter. There was always this smell of fresh air, oranges and biltong. That was definitely my happy place.

'Now imagine that 'happy place' when you go back into the tunnel', my mom said.

The second time I went into the tunnel I was more relaxed, although it still felt as if there was no oxygen. I just kept thinking of my 'happy place'. I closed my eyes and breathed in deeply.

The 10 minutes in the tunnel felt like hours to me. The whole time I was in there I had no idea what they were testing me for. Time passed and they finally pulled me out.

'I don't ever want to do that again, Mommy. Will you make sure of that, please?'

She promised me that I would never have to do the CAT scan again. Little did I know that the CAT scan would be the least of my problems when it came to medical tests.

When CMT is suspected, the physician may order electro-diagnostic tests and these were next on his agenda. The testing process consists of two parts: nerve conduction studies and electromyography (EMG). During the nerve conduction studies, electrodes are placed on the skin over a peripheral motor or sensory nerve. These produce a small electric shock that may cause mild discomfort. The electrical impulse stimulates sensory and motor nerves and provides quantifiable information that the doctor can use to arrive at a diagnosis. EMG involves inserting a needle electrode through the skin to measure the bioelectrical activity of muscles. Specific abnormalities in the readings signify axon degeneration. EMG may be useful in further characterising the distribution and severity of peripheral nerve involvement.

Next to come was an electro-diagnostic test. They put electrodes around my fingers, which sent impulses through my nervous system. It was painful and I did not like it at all. When they finished the test on my right hand, I didn't want them to continue with the test on my left hand. After they explained how important the test was, I gave in.

They then took a patella hammer and hit me on my kneecap.

'Why would you hit me with a hammer? Are you crazy?' I asked the lady doing the test.

'I'm testing your neuron responses,' she replied.

'What the hell is a neuron?' I thought to myself. Half of the jargon they used that day made no sense at all to me.

Next they made me stand on one leg to test my balance. I fell over. I was scared that they might think I was drunk as I had seen on TV how that they make people stand on one leg to test this.

When the day finally ended, I asked my mom why that test was necessary.

'Is it really so important to you that I walk on my heels, Mommy?'

'It's not about you being able to walk on your heels, my darling. All of the tests you are going through will make sense to you soon. You might be very sick my child', she responded.

Sick? I didn't feel sick. Why would my mom think I was sick?

When my parents received the results, I could see that they were very worried. However, the doctors in the city were unfortunately not able to give a diagnosis. They instead referred us to a specialist in City in the North.

After that day I realised that I might be sick, that something was seriously wrong with me. We had travelled to City in the North before as my uncle and aunt lived there. We used to visit them regularly and I had good memories of fun times at their home. Our families would get together and the cousins would play and swim for hours in my uncle's lovely swimming pool. We usually visited them in summer and in winter we would sometimes go to the Kruger National Park with them. Those holidays with my uncle and aunt in the Kruger Park were the best ever!

However, this visit, was different as I would have to go to the doctor. All I was interested in at that time was knowing whether there would be more tests. I didn't ask my parents how far it still was to City in the North, I repeatedly asked them if they were sure there would be no more tests.

My parents' response was subtle but not straightforward and after asking the same question for the fifth time, I realised that they did not know the answer to my question. They didn't want to say anything that might upset me.

I was scared. I became nauseous. I didn't know what was going on or what to expect. I knew that I was sick. What I didn't know was how sick 'not being able to walk on your heels' can make you.

When the day arrived for my doctor's appointment in City in the North, I was beyond scared. My stomach was upset. I had headaches and really felt sick. In the doctor's waiting room I started to shiver. 'If 'they' say I'm sick, I have to look and feel sick,' I decided.

'Miss Grobler?' The receptionist called my name. I went into the examination room. The doctor was old and grey, very friendly and had ice cold hands. He started with a few questions:

To make a diagnosis of CMT they begin by taking a standard medical history, family history, and then doing a thorough neurological examination. The patient is asked about the nature and duration of their symptoms and whether other family members have the disease. During the neurological examination, the physician looks for evidence of muscle weakness in the arms, legs, hands and feet, decreased muscle bulk, reduced tendon reflexes, and sensory loss. Doctors look for evidence of foot deformities, such as high arches, hammertoes, inverted heels or flat feet. Other orthopaedic problems, such as mild scoliosis or hip dysplasia, may also be evident. A specific symptom that may be found in people with CMT1 is nerve enlargement that can be felt, or even seen, through the skin. These enlarged nerves, known as hypertrophic nerves, are caused by abnormally thickened myelin sheaths.

'Why doesn't he listen to my heart like other doctors do when I'm sick', I wondered?

He touched my legs and hands and asked me to make different movements. I was not able to do some of those he told me to do when he touched my feet.

'Am I supposed to be able to do that?' I asked the doctor.

'Yes, my dear,' the doctor replied with a smile on his face.

He left the room. I sat on the bed with my feet hanging down and tried again to do the movements he had earlier asked me to do. I couldn't. I got frustrated and irritated.

'Why can't I do those movements, Dad?'

My dad looked at my uncle. My uncle responded by saying that the doctor would be able to tell us soon. He told me not to worry, that everything would be fine.

The doctor came back into the room and gave us the news. He explained many things that I wasn't able to understand. But I could understand enough to know that everything was *not* fine.

'Charcot-Marie-Tooth'[1], the doctor said.

My first thoughts were about who Marie was and what was wrong with her tooth?

Dad asked the doctor to explain the illness to us, in a way that we could understand and to tell us what to-do to make it better.

The doctor responded; 'Genetic testing is available for some types of CMT and results are usually enough to confirm a diagnosis. In addition, genetic counselling is available to assist people to understand their condition and plan for the future.

If all the diagnostic work-up is inconclusive or genetic testing comes back negative, a neurologist can perform a nerve biopsy to confirm the diagnosis. This involves removing a small piece of peripheral nerve through an incision in the skin. This is most often done by removing a piece of the nerve that runs down the calf. The nerve is then examined under a microscope. Individuals with CMT1 typically show signs of abnormal myelination, specifically, 'onion bulb' where formations may be seen that represent axons surrounded by layers of demyelinated and demyelinating Schwann cells. Individuals with CMT1 will usually show signs of axon degeneration. Recently, skin biopsy has been used to study unmyelinated and myelinated nerve fibres in a minimally invasive way but their clinical use in CMT has not yet been established.

There is no cure for CMT but physical therapy, occupational therapy, braces and other orthopaedic devices, and even orthopaedic surgery, can help individuals cope with the disabling symptoms of the disease. In addition, painkillers can be prescribed for individuals who have severe pain.'

He went on to explain that physical and occupational therapy, the preferred treatment for CMT, involves muscle strength training, muscle and ligament stretching, stamina training, and moderate aerobic exercise. Most therapists recommend a specialised treatment program, designed in consultation and with the approval of the person's physician, to fit individual abilities and needs. Therapists also suggest entering into a treatment program as early as possible as muscle strengthening might delay or reduce muscle atrophy. Thus strength training is most useful if it begins before nerve degeneration and muscle weakness progress to the point of disability.

---

[1] **Charcot–Marie–Tooth disease (CMT)**, also known as **Charcot–Marie–Tooth neuropathy**, and **peroneal muscular atrophy** is one of the hereditary motor and sensory neuropathies, a group of varied inherited disorders of the peripheral nervous system characterised by progressive loss of muscle tissue and touch sensation across various parts of the body. Currently incurable, this disease is the most commonly inherited neurological disorder, and affects approximately 1 in 2,500 people. CMT was previously classified as a subtype of muscular dystrophy. - https://en.wikipedia.org/wiki/Charcot%E2%80%93Marie%E2%80%93Tooth_disease

Stretching may also prevent or reduce joint deformities that can result from uneven muscle pull on bones. Exercises to help build stamina or increase endurance can help prevent the fatigue that results from performing everyday activities that require strength and mobility. Moderate aerobic activity can help to maintain cardiovascular fitness and overall health. Most therapists recommend low-impact or no-impact exercises, such as cycling or swimming, rather than activities such as walking or jogging, which may put stress on fragile muscles and joints.

Many CMT patients require ankle braces and other orthopaedic devices to maintain everyday mobility and prevent injury. Ankle braces can help to prevent ankle sprains by providing support and stability during activities such as walking or climbing stairs. High-top shoes or boots can also provide support for weak ankles. Thumb splints can help with hand weakness and loss of fine motor skills. It is suggested that assistive devices be used before disability sets in because the devices may prevent muscle strain and reduce muscle weakening. Some individuals with CMT have orthopaedic surgery to reverse foot and joint deformities.

The neuropathy of CMT affects both motor and sensory nerves. (Motor nerves cause muscles to contract and also control voluntary muscle activity, such as speaking, walking, breathing, and swallowing.) A typical symptom includes weakness of the foot and lower leg muscles, which may result in foot drop and a high-stepped gait with frequent tripping or falls. Foot deformities, such as high arches and hammertoes (a condition in which the middle joint of a toe bends upward) are also characteristic due to weakness of the small muscles in the feet. In addition, the lower legs may take on an 'inverted champagne bottle' appearance due to the loss of muscle bulk. Later in the disease, weakness and muscle atrophy may occur in the hands, resulting in difficulty carrying out fine motor skills (the coordination of small movements usually in the fingers, hands, wrists, feet, and tongue).

The onset of symptoms most often occurs in adolescence or early adulthood but some individuals develop symptoms in mid-adulthood. The severity of symptoms varies greatly among individuals and even among family members who all have the disease. Progression of symptoms is gradual. Pain can range from mild to severe and some people may need to rely on foot or leg braces or other orthopaedic devices to maintain mobility. Although rare, in some cases individuals may have respiratory muscle weakness. CMT is not considered a fatal disease and people with most forms of CMT have a normal life expectancy. Nerve cells communicate information to distant targets in the body by sending electrical signals down a long, thin part of the cell, the axon. In order to increase the speed at which these electrical signals travel, the axon is insulated by myelin, which is produced by another type of cell called the Schwann cell. Myelin twists around the axon like a Swiss-roll cake and prevents the loss of electrical signals. Without an intact axon and myelin sheath, peripheral nerve cells are unable to activate target muscles or to relay sensory information from the limbs back to the brain.

CMT is caused by mutations in genes that produce proteins involved in the structure and function of either the peripheral nerve axon or the myelin sheath. Although different proteins are abnormal in different forms of CMT disease, all of the mutations affect the normal functioning of the peripheral nerves. Consequently, these nerves slowly degenerate and lose the ability to communicate with their distant targets. The degeneration of motor nerves results in muscle weakness and atrophy in the extremities (arms, legs, hands or feet) and, in some cases, the degeneration of sensory nerves results in a reduced ability to feel heat, cold, and pain.

The gene mutations in CMT disease are usually inherited. Each of us normally possess two copies of every gene, one inherited from each parent. Some forms of CMT are inherited in an autosomal dominant fashion, which means that only one copy of the abnormal gene is needed to cause the disease. Other forms of CMT are inherited in an autosomal recessive fashion, which means that both copies of the abnormal gene must be present to cause the disease. Still other forms of CMT are inherited in an X-linked fashion, which means that the abnormal gene is located on the X chromosome. The X and Y chromosomes determine an individual's sex. Individuals with two X chromosomes are female and individuals with one X and one Y chromosome are male.

In rare cases, the gene mutation causing CMT disease is a new, spontaneously occurring mutation in the individual's genetic material and has not been passed down through the family.

After all of that information, I was shattered. Remember that I was only 11 years old. I started crying. My dad and my uncle both started crying too.

'What am I supposed to do now,' I thought? 'I'm sick and I am going to be in a wheelchair soon'. At that point we did not fully understand what was happening and what the doctor's explanation meant. I was not interested in more detail. To my understanding, I would not be able to walk and the only form of exercise I would be able to do would be cycling or swimming. I liked both those sports but was more interested in team sports. I wanted to play netball.

'My life is over and I am useless,' I thought in despair. 'No more sport and no more friends. I'm a cripple, a pathetic loser.' I went quiet for a while. I went into deep depression and didn't know what to do or what to expect from life. I didn't know if I would be able to finish school or go to university. I only heard the bad things the doctor said about the disease. At that stage I did not know how to filter the news and if it meant I would be able to have a normal life.

I made up my mind that I would not be able to do anything and needed to accept it. I needed to become more academic and focus on excelling in my school work. This despite the fact that I didn't like homework or studying at all. It was hard for me to sit still and study. I would rather play outside or play sports.

I gave up on life, because I believed life had given up on me. When I was still young, I often asked my mother why God had decided to give me this disease. What did I do wrong? Was I a naughty girl? I used to pray and ask God to make me better. Most nights when I prayed, I would ask Him to heal me. 'I want to be normal, God; I want to be like all the other kids. I want to be able to walk on my heels, God. I want to run and play with my friends. Why would you do this to me, God? I don't deserve this.'

I grew up......

If only I had known then what I know today. I would have stopped asking God for reasons why He made me the way I am. Today I thank Him for the blessing of this disease. I would never have been who I am today if I did not have this disease. I would also never have met the people that I have if I did not have CMT. When people ask if they can pray for me to be healed and to walk normally, I tell them that I am normal. I'm happy with the way I walk. I'm happy that God made me the way I am. I am unique, I have a life for which I am thankful. Rather pray for people with life-threatening diseases such as cancer.

God made me with a 'funny walk' so that I could inspire people and live life to the fullest. Most of all, He used it to teach me not to take life for granted but rather, to live life according to my own normal.

Chapter Two

Early Days

I was a challenge not only to myself but also to my parents, teachers and the people who worked with me. My parents worried about the choices I would make in my life. With my condition having been diagnosed, they did not know what I would be able to do or how I would experience life. On that day in the hospital room, they simply saw their innocent little girl starting her new life.

My parents had not wanted to wait too long before trying for a second child as they wanted my brother to have a friend to play with. When my mother asked him whether he would prefer a brother or a sister, he always said that he wanted a sister. Although I sometimes wonder what it would have been like to have had a sister, as a small child this didn't bother me too much as Sias and I were good friends. When I went to boarding school though, the support only a sister can provide would have been invaluable. However, I will never trade the things I learnt from my brother in for anything in the world. His passion to be the best at everything he does continues to be an inspiration to me.

Where and how I grew up had a great influence on my life and on the choices I made. From a very young age I was determined to do everything that I could possibly do; to play as much as I could and to laugh more than the average person does. Research shows that children laugh more than 300 times a day but that as an adult, you laugh less than 20 times a day. The reason for this is that people somehow become too serious as they get older and lose the ability to laugh. Adults should try to regain the joy of childhood by becoming more playful and humorous. I certainly think that adults are often far too serious and would definitely benefit from laughing more often, although I have not been able to find scientific evidence to prove this.

What I do know is that my parents were happy; they were content with their lives and they were ready to have children. The joyful way my mother interacted with me made me a happy baby and

I still think she laughed twice as much as I did. As a result of her attitude, I adopted a culture of positivity and I laugh a lot. Most people I meet or interact with can vouch for that; I always look for ways to get people to smile.

Laughter is contagious; the more you laugh when you interact with your child or with people around you, the more *they* will laugh. Imagine a world filled with smiles and happy faces; people would be so much happier and also more patient.

Laugh with the world and the world will laugh with you.

Playful

'Be the person your dog thinks you are.'
My brother, Sias, was very protective of me from the day I was born. I still smile when I think back on how the two of us played and did fun things on our farm. He is two years older than I am and we were the fittest and naughtiest kids imaginable and would play catch for hours on end. 'Cowboys and Crooks' was our favourite game and we would transform our world into an amazing make-believe one. We built farms in the sand and watered the make-believe fields that we'd designed. We used to walk into and roll our toes in the mud and loved the feeling when it squished through our toes. My mother struggled to get us to come inside to eat lunch and in the evenings she battled to get us to come home. Her voice was like an intercom. 'Tai-Tai!' she would call for my brother. If he did not answer, she would call my name, 'Poplap!'....

We would take our time getting home; we would first finish what we were busy with and then grudgingly make our way home. My mum soon learnt our ways and started calling us 15 minutes before she wanted us to be ready for meals.

We hated bathing but Mum had to make sure we washed every night because we got so filthy playing in sand, mud and on the grass. When I got into the bath, my entire body would sting from the grass burns I'd gotten from falling and from crawling on my knees. What more could an active child ask for?

My parents loved giving us nicknames and we knew when they used these, that everything was fine. If my mother called me by my full name, Serijke, I would immediately know that something was wrong or that I was in trouble. My dad used to call me 'Dollie pop' because of my long, golden-blonde hair. He said my face looked like that of a doll.

We started playing early every morning and stayed outside from sunrise to sunset. Barefoot was the *only* way to be! Getting us to put shoes on would depend on how loudly my mother spoke to us.

I had dolls but rarely played 'dress-up' as I found it very boring. My brother thought the same and, therefore, decided one day to show me how to cut and style my Barbie's hair. After a week I asked him when her hair would grow back and he told me to be patient as it would take time. I'm still waiting...

On Sunday afternoons it was important for my parents to take a long nap. We would eat so much at lunch that it would be almost impossible to keep our eyes open after the meal. As my parents went off to have their nap, my brother would slip out to go and play outside. As he protectively didn't want me to get into trouble, he would tell me that there was a monster under my bed. If I got off my bed, it would catch me. I believed him and for two hours I wouldn't move or make a noise and just sat on my bed, imagining the shape and size of this monster. The most important thing that we had to remember was not to wake our parents up! Come hell or high water, you did *not* want to anger Dad. He had spent a long week working hard and really treasured his Sunday naps. As I got older, my brother relented and would take me with on his Sunday afternoon adventures. It was fun, yet also scary and we would play in silence for hours.

We had no electricity during the day and my dad only started the generator engine in the evenings when we needed light in the house. We had a television but it was definitely not for us children. Dad would watch the news and then my parents watched *MacGyver*, *Airwolf* or *Knight Rider* (the talking car) together. I can still remember *Airwolf* and *Chips* and *Dallas* were also favourites of theirs.

In those days televisions did not come with remote controls, the children were the remote. If my dad wanted the TV louder, he would ask my brother or me to adjust the volume. And the same procedure if he wanted it turned down again. There was only one TV channel, thank goodness for that. Just imagine how many times I would have had to get up and down if my dad had wanted to do some channel surfing! I would have been as fit as a fiddle.

Haas Das, *Wielie Walie* and *Brakenjan* were the only programmes we children were allowed to watch. Our favourite programs started at 18h00 and this assisted my mother to get us home before dark. *Heidi* was my favourite children's story and I used to love watching Heidi and her lamb having the time of their lives playing together in the mountains. *Brakenjan* was an animated series about a dog that was a musketeer and fought enemies in every episode. I loved the animations and as I also love dogs, this brave, colourfully drawn hound kept my attention from start to finish.

I believe that the best way to teach a person how to love and care is by giving them a dog. I cannot remember a time in my life when I did not have a dog.

10 reasons to have a dog:

- A dog is always happy to see you;
- A dog never talks back;
- A dog will love you unconditionally;
- A dog will never cheat on you;
- Dogs will keep you fit – so walk your dog regularly;
- Dogs feel sick when you are sick;
- Dogs want love through touching and stroking – nothing more;
- Dogs will never lie to you;
- Dogs warn you when there is danger and will protect you;
- Dogs depend on you for their survival.

In return, all a dog wants from you is for you to love and care for it. They need you to feed them and to pick up their poop.

We kept 35 dogs on our farm as my dad used the dogs to help hunt. We had Dalmatians, Jack Russell's, Whippets and Blue ticks. When I was 16 years old, we got our first Dachshund, Samuel. In 2011 Sammy died at the age of 14 and although he'd been deaf and could no longer see properly, he was sorely missed. When my mother got home from town one day, she didn't see Sammy in the driveway, where he usually waited. He did not hear or see my mother coming into the driveway and she accidentally drove over her own doggie. She was devastated by Sammy's death and grieved for months. I reacted in the same way whenever I lost one of my dogs, I would grieve for years. Each dog has their own unique personality and for dog lovers, one dog can never replace another.

Dogs taught me valuable life lessons. A dog is like a child to me, the child that I thought I would never have. Until April 2015…but you will have to read the book to find out what happened then.

The Good Old Days

Without electricity, the farmers had a unique way of generating power. The kitchen on our farm was a massive one and I loved spending time there with my mother. The AGA stove was always on so the kitchen stayed warm. An AGA stove is a cast iron storage stove and cooker that can absorb heat from a relatively low-intensity heat source, which was mostly slow burning coal or wood. The AGA stove was invented in 1922 by the Swedish Nobel Prize winner, Nils Gustaf

Dalén. Another person I believe deserves a Nobel Prize is my resourceful, tender-hearted mother, who made all the food for our household and the workers on the farm on her trusty AGA. She even dried our school clothes in the lower oven and during the winter, Mum would get up before us to heat our clothes on the stove so they would be lovely and warm when we put them on. She also baked the best rusks in that oven and still does even today. Unfortunately for us, she now has to bake them with an Eskom-dependant electric stove. I used to love her 'krummelpap' with Aromat and butter' in my younger days. Pork scratchings, better known as 'Kiaings' and kidneys was and still is my favourite meal. The way everything operated on the farm was very energy-efficient.

The iron was heated on a gas stove, which we also used when we went camping. The old irons are still on the farm but are no longer used. You could use those heavy cast irons as a weapon or more safely, as a door stop. They are so heavy that you could develop tennis elbow from ironing with one of them. There were no washing machines or dishwashers on the farm in those days, everything was done by hand.

My mother used to have four ladies working for her on the farm, and each worker had specific chores to attend to. The farm workers were provided with a house and their food. The farmers employed and generated work for a huge proportion of the Free State population and our workers seemed to love working on the farm. The only dilemma that they had in those days was getting a proper education for their children. There was a school in the area but most of the children started working at a very young age so did not get many years of schooling. The education they did get was of a poor standard in the smaller community schools. The farm workers definitely fell into the category of 'previously disadvantaged' groups when it came to education.

It was not difficult or hard work for the farmers to use what they had to generate power to make food. The primitive way they used to generate electricity was extremely environmentally friendly. As the world evolved, the farmers had to evolve with it and as electricity became available to the farmers, they started using it. Not because they wanted to but because they had to as it became more expensive to buy coal and gas than to buy electricity. The world forced them into a direction that they didn't necessarily want to go.

One night at about 21h00, I followed my dad when he went outside to switch off the engine that generated our electricity. It was pitch dark outside and I didn't have a torch with me. There were three steps going up to the engine room. I walked up the stairs and stopped on the second step to watch how my dad switched the engine off. He turned around and flashed his torch in my eyes. The bright light blinded me and I couldn't see my dad's face. I just heard his tremulous voice telling me to stand still.

'Don't look down and do *not* move a finger,' he said. Before I could even think of looking down he tackled me. Full blown and with an incredible force we went flying through the air. As we landed, I was lying on top of my dad. I didn't know what had hit me; but he must have turned around in the air to save me from injury. He looked scared and I could feel that his heart was beating fast.

'What's wrong Daddy?' I asked.

He looked at me and said, 'There was a big snake lying between your legs when you were standing on the steps, Dollie pop'. The Cape Cobra that he had seen between my legs was getting ready to protect itself and if I had moved one inch to either the left or right, I would have stepped onto it. One bite from that Cape Cobra would have brought me to the final 45 minutes of my life. Fortunately my dad saved me from that moderately sized but highly venomous reptile!

After that incident, I never went to the engine room again at night and until today I am still scared of snakes. My mom had always warned us to watch out for snakes, especially in summer when snakes come out of hibernation and one is more likely to cross paths with them. I've had many encounters with snakes on the farm but the Cape Cobra incident was thankfully the closest I have come to being bitten by one of these creatures.

Creating New Opportunities

Technology has affected society in a number of ways and has changed life in the farming community in many ways. Electrical appliances coming into our homes meant that farmers didn't need as many farm workers as they used to and many people lost their jobs as a result of technological changes. I'm a strong believer in creating job opportunities for domestic workers and I still have a domestic worker who I love very much. She ensures that our house is clean and our clothes are ironed. She washes the dishes by hand in order to save electricity and water. Not only is she saving us money in this way but she is also helping to save the world. South Africa is currently struggling to generate and provide sufficient electricity for the country's needs and is in a position where the supplier sometimes has to do 'load shedding' to save electricity. We *Homo sapiens* have the ability to destroy or control our world and environment. If we reflect on what humans have done to our world over the past millennia, we can clearly see that we destroy our natural resources. Why can't we just use electricity and water sparingly? Why is it necessary to control our power usage with a load shedding schedule?

We all need to constantly be looking for ways in which to conserve power. All lights, appliances, stoves and heaters should be switched off when a warning is broadcast on TV in times of high power usage. How many people actually take note of that warning and do actually switch their appliances off when they see it?

Our country has run out of resources to provide everyone with sufficient power and when you look at the newest appliances available, it will come as no surprise that the trusty AGA stove is back on the market. Are we going back to the way things were 30 years ago? The scary thing is that it took the human race only 30 years to use up so many of our natural resources. With pollution, fires, preservatives, technology and crime, we are rapidly damaging our planet.

Climate change is a reality and the seasons are changing; summer is becoming hotter, and winter colder. Tornadoes are causing great damage in America and floods and fires create havoc in parts of Australia. Drought is making farming very difficult for South African farmers and at times floods wipe out their crops.

Do you think that the end of the world could be upon us?

Global warming is a real issue. Wildlife protection groups focus on saving the rhino. Animals are becoming extinct and next on the endangered species list are the black rhino and the African Wild Dog. Humans are the reason for this— our species, *Homo sapiens*, is selfish. We take and take and don't give anything back. Everything is always about ourselves, about what we can get and what we can achieve or be. Very rarely do we operate from a perspective of what we can do to make the world better. As Albert Einstein, in all his scientific glory once said, 'Our task must be to free ourselves… by widening our circle of compassion to embrace all living creatures and the whole of nature and its beauty.'

Rhino poaching occurs mostly because the rhino horn is used in traditional medicines and healing in the Asian world. Poachers are being paid millions for precious rhino horn and are brutally killing rhino just for their horns. It takes a rhino 16 months to produce offspring and only takes one shot from a poacher's gun to kill this beautiful animal.

I have had a passion for nature and animals from a very young age and I still get upset when I hear about rhino poaching, whale hunting, animal abuse and global warming. I get angry but I also feel disappointed in myself for not doing anything about these issues.

Where do we start? The answer is simple. 'With yourself.'

We are *Homo sapiens*. We discover, we destroy and we can survive. Humans control humans by creating rules and regulations, we manage each other but still do not like to be told what to do or not to do.

Caring

In those days the best way in which we could communicate was via the telephone or 'snail mail.' What I mean by 'snail mail' is mail being sent via the postal system. We used to write letters to our friends and families and had to plan for people's birthdays. Writing and sending a birthday card needed to be done two weeks before the actual birthday to ensure it arrived on time. We used to invite many friends and family members to join us to celebrate our birthdays, a celebration of life and another year. In the modern era, we are lucky to get a message on Social media, or a happy birthday on a WhatsApp group as most of applications (apps) remind you when it is someone's birthday. No longer do we plan ahead and get excited about an upcoming birthday, we have lost the sense of personal contact and caring. Life became faster and we think we are becoming smarter but if it means losing our sense of being tender, kind-hearted and caring, are we really? The world today is more populated than ever before and we can communicate with others from anywhere on the globe, yet many people today are lonelier than ever before. When was the last time you sent somebody a birthday card? When was the last time you phoned someone to say 'Merry Christmas'? Or do you just forward a message that someone else forwarded to you, to all your friends and family? It seems to me that we are losing the sense of the personal touch as we become more technologically advanced.

We always had fun with telephones back then. Every town had a switchboard operating system and when you wanted to phone from the farm, you had to pick up the handset and enquire, 'Number busy?' If there was no response, you could then dial the switchboard. The operator would say: 'Number, please?' You had to give the name of the town and the number that you wanted to dial and the operator would dial it for you. While you were busy with your conversation, you could sometimes hear that the operator was listening in on your call. We didn't care that much, because we also used to listen to what our neighbours had to say on their telephone calls. The town switchboard operators were also the local information centre to catch-up on all the gossip of the town. If somebody wanted to know anything about anyone else, they would ask them. I think being an operator back in those days must have been a powerful job! There was a very humorous TV programme called *Nommer Asseblief* (Number Please) based on the lives of these switchboard operators. Gossip kept the people going and even today gossip is everywhere, at home, at work, between friends and even in churches.

When our ancestors discovered language billions of years ago, it was a way in which to communicate with each other and to express feelings. The 'cave men' not only used language to warn each other of danger but also to gossip and express their feelings. If you think about it logically, do you think cave men spoke about how their business was going, or about the next best thing? I don't think so and am pretty sure they rather gossiped about who was sleeping with who and how bad the last hunt had gone because of that one guy who couldn't use his spear properly. Gossip is the one thing that has not become extinct or endangered over millions of years of evolution.

Inventing language not only gave *Homo sapiens* an advantage in everyday life, it also put our species at the top of the food chain. Language gave us the power to express ourselves in the same way as fire gave us the power to control and telephones gave us power to communicate on a level that had not been possible for billions of years before.

We used to phone our friends and families on birthdays, Christmas, New Year, when someone was ill or to mark any special occasion. A few years ago we would have spoken for too long on the phone because phone calls were also not that expensive in those days. To receive a phone call from someone can be uplifting, can make you feel loved or even just be a plain and simple gesture of caring. In today's world you can count yourself lucky if you receive an electronic message or a generic e-card wishing you 'Happy birthday!'

The world changes and we have to change with it. Change is good we are told and the sooner we adapt the sooner we can move forward. For many years, Christmas was a really important time for people and we really made an effort to make time for our families and to buy them presents. As we approached Christmas, I became more and more excited about what I would give to who and I also wondered what people would give me for Christmas. Christmas today is not what it used to be when I was younger and people are not buying gifts anymore because it has become too expensive to do so. Most people say that it is costs too much to buy presents for everyone. Have we lost the sense of giving? Is it really about the price of the present?

Christmas is about celebrating the birth of Jesus Christ and the meaning of the presents can differ for everyone reading this book. To me it is important to give gifts to other people as what you give, you will receive, perhaps not in the form of presents but maybe at work, in love or in friendliness. When I was a child my mother always made sure there were many presents around the Christmas tree. She made sure there was a Father Christmas and also that we experienced the Christmas spirit and gave to others on that one day of the year. This year my mother told me that she was not going to buy presents because the rest of the family was not doing so. I told her that the values she had instilled in us were to always give presents to everyone on Christmas Day, irrespective of whether we would receive something in return. Why would she want to change in accordance with what the world has become?

It is important to stick with what you believe. If it is in your values to give something small to someone for Christmas, do it. If they don't give you something, accept that. Everyone has different values and perspectives, don't let the world dictate what yours should be. Don't get angry and stop giving, be who you are. For me it is the most exciting thing to see the expressions on the faces of my family when they open their presents. I love Christmas!

The eating and drinking that goes with the day is also really special to me. My mother makes all my favourite foods which vary from gammon, roast lamb, salads and the most delicious puddings.

I can remember how, as children, we would be so stuffed from all the delicious food that we would just sleep afterwards. I still do it, I eat so much over Christmas that I feel as if I want to burst.

Many years ago people would travel far distances to meet with their families to wish them a Merry Christmas. When travelling became too expensive and dangerous, people started posting cards to each other for this purpose. Then the cards became old-fashioned and people started phoning each other on Christmas Day. Nowadays people will post a group chat message to wish people Merry Christmas or alternatively send a SMS.

Change is ugly in the beginning, messy in the middle but beautiful in the end. As technology changes the world, we can either adapt to it or we can stay who we are. Be yourself because everyone else is taken. Live *your* values and do what is important to you.

Trust and Love

When I think back to when I was a little girl, life seemed easier and far less complicated.
My dad says that when my brother left for boarding school, I became a real farm girl. Wherever he went, I would go with him. I used to love the fields, the sheep and being outdoors; I was a real busybody when it came to farming. I have learnt so much about nature and how we should treasure it. God gave us this wonderful world and we need to look after it, because the world is good to us. The world and nature provide food and all our essential needs. I believe that we take this for granted and that we should have respect for our world. That respect needs to start with ourselves as we can't expect someone to have respect for the world, if they do not first have respect for themselves.

Many farmers are leaving South Africa because they don't see a future for farming in the country. I'm a strong believer that if you choose to see no future for yourself and your family, you will have no future. Your success and future depend on how badly you want to be successful and to live the life that you want. People always think that the grass is greener on the other side yet the reality is that it will be exactly the same elsewhere as in South Africa because it will still be you making the decisions. You are in control of your own actions and decisions. I love South Africa. Our country has beautiful, fertile fields and our farms have such great potential.

As a little girl I would become bored very quickly. My dad bought a brand new baby blue car with red lines down its sides. I didn't think much of the red lines, to me they were just another thing that needed to be removed. So remove them I did, with my small kiddies' hands and little fingers. I scratched the lines off, bit by bit. I was curious to see what happened when I removed the red lines and I found out when my dad became furious with me. I learnt another valuable lesson that day, don't touch your dad's brand new car!

When he bought his new pick-up truck, I wanted to leave him a message to congratulate him on it. So I took a piece of wire and, because I couldn't yet write, I drew him a smiley face on the roof of the truck with the wire. The marks are still engraved on the roof of that pick-up truck, the same truck that my dad thought me to drive in.

I was only four years old when I started driving. I was too small to reach the foot pedals so my dad had to put me on his lap. Dad would change the gears and I handled the steering wheel. It was an amazing experience for a little girl! On the farm we children were only allowed to drive on a certain road from one gate to the next. My dad didn't want to take any chances on roads with lots of turns and hills but wanted to keep the driving simple for me. As I grew older, he would send me around the farm in his truck to do little jobs for him. The first time I drove on my own was really challenging as I still couldn't see over the steering wheel and had to look between the steering wheel and the dashboard. My feet hardly reached the pedals but I was determined to drive that pick-up truck. I did drive the truck that day and on many days after that. My dad was, and still is, the best teacher in the world. The trust he showed in allowing me to drive his truck taught me not to be scared to trust other people, or your own child. Being trusted teaches us not to try to control and steer everything in everyone's lives.

I thought it was very sweet of me to do that drawing on the roof of the truck for him but my dad started crying from anger. Or were they happy tears?

He seldom got angry when I was little and my parents both taught me great values. Trust and love yourself first, before you can trust and love others. When I employ people today, I trust them 100% from day one, until they disappoint me. It can take years to build trust but it can take just a minute to break that trust down. That's why it is so important to keep your good name. Live every day as if you want to keep the trust of others.

I felt loved and safe and feel I need to elaborate a little more on the 'safe'. The farmhouse is really big and at night it becomes a very scary place for a little girl. It has high ceilings, cold eight foot walls and wooden floors. The passages are long and dark with a red carpet, if you stand at the one end you can't see the other end of the passage. I used to go to bed early every night and on some nights my mom was allowed to switch the lights off. On others I would be very scared and she had to leave the door open and the lights on. I would call her five or six times during the nights on which I was scared. One night I heard steps in the corridor; the wooden floors made a creaking sound. When the lights were off, my room was pitch dark. There were no street or city lights nearby to cast a shadow in the room.

I was woken by the same creaking sound of footsteps in the corridor and when I opened my eyes, I could see a man's figure next to my bed. When I switched the light on, there was nothing. I strongly believed that this was a ghost. The farm workers told me that a man had committed suicide on the farm and they believed that his soul never left the house and that it was haunted. A farmhouse in the middle of nowhere… To a five year-old girl, this story was believable and very scary. I would be lying if I said that I no longer believe it. I still get shivers down my spine when I walk down those passages. My babysitter named the ghost 'Lobo' and my mother also used the name to scare me into eating my vegetables.

In those days my mom would come and tickle my back to calm me down. She would tell me that everything would be fine and that the noises were caused by the wood expanding and shrinking. In winter it would shrink from the cold and in the summer it would expand from the heat. When I asked my mom about Lobo when I was older, she told me that she had also been scared.

As an adult I still miss the days where I could just call my mother or father and they could make all my troubles and worries go away.

We live in a very fast-paced world today and it's a case of 'Keep up or the world will swallow you.' Most of us experience more stress than we can handle. One day you may feel you have it under control and the next you may feel that you have no control whatsoever. *There are very few emotional states to be in more dangerous than that of stress but my advice to you is to think of what a privilege it is to be alive when you get up every morning, to breathe, to think, to enjoy life and to love. As the quote from Boethius goes, 'Nothing is miserable unless you think it so; and on the other hand, nothing brings happiness unless you are content with it.'*

Chapter Three

Curiosity

At age six I had to go to boarding school in a very small town. I was excited and scared at the same time about this new adventure in my life and I can remember getting dressed to go to my new school on the first day of the term. My mother tied my long blonde hair into two neat pigtails and I asked her, 'Who will do my hair in the mornings at school?' She told me that I would make friends who would help me. I started to cry as I didn't know how to make friends. Growing up on a farm I had only gone to pre-school once a week and there were only three of us in the class. On the farm I used to play with my brother and the farm workers' children so hadn't had much opportunity to make other friends.

What if the friends I made could not do my hair properly? Then I would have to go to school with messy hair. I was so distracted worrying about my hair that I wasn't thinking about school and thoughts of being lonely there didn't even cross my mind.

I also didn't think about the fact that my parents would not be there to help me with homework or to tuck me into bed at night. I was just focussed on how I wanted my mom to do my hair in the mornings, I wanted my hair to be done the way *she* had always done it every morning for the past six years. It felt as if she was pushing me away to stand on my own two feet and that I was way too young to be independent.

My school dress was way too long as my mom had ensured she could adjust it when I grew taller. My school bag was huge, or at least it felt huge to me. When I look back now I realise that the suitcase was really of a quite normal size, it just seemed huge to me. I was going to the same boarding school that my brother attended and that was the one thing I was excited about. I would now see him every day instead of waiting for him to come home on Fridays. It wasn't long before I realised that I missed my parents and home so much, that I again started longing for Fridays to arrive.

The school was small and there were only two children in grade 1 (or Sub A as it was still called in those days). This made making friends rather difficult as I didn't have many options. In my hostel dormitory, I shared with girls who were three to four years older than I was.

Life in the hostel was controlled by bells. The first bell that rang in the morning was the wake-up call bell, 30 minutes later the second bell rang and that's when you had to sit on your bed and read your Bible. I couldn't read yet but my parents had taught me how to pray so I would pray instead of reading. I prayed the same thing every day, an Afrikaans verse that my mom had taught me. It was a pattern prayer in which you first thank God for your mom and dad and then ask Him to send rain. You followed that by asking for help and guidance to assist you through the day and last but not least, you prayed for the soldiers fighting for our country.

The third bell was for breakfast. When it had gone off, we would all go and stand in a queue outside the dining room and the person in charge of inspection that day would then walk along the line and check if our shoes were clean and our hair neat and tidy. You were not allowed to talk or make any noise while waiting in the queue and when you walked into the dining room, you could see the kids drooling for their food. While the hostel head said grace, the older kids started grabbing bread and porridge while the other children's eyes were closed for the prayer. I soon picked up on this trend of not closing my eyes during prayer. Keep your eyes open and grab food! If you didn't do that, you would go hungry.

I'm still grateful to all the girls I shared a room with in grade 1. They not only showed me how to do my hair but also made sure that I was awake, dressed, and ready to go to school every morning. They made sure that I ate and that I was well looked after. To call them friends would be an understatement as they were more like my mentors. I had to grow up very quickly at a very young age and fortunately had a great support structure in these girls who really cared about me. I got my nickname, "Siekie."

When I asked her why she chose that particular nickname for me, she said that I was quiet yet filled with self-confidence. She also said I had adapted quickly to my surroundings but the main reason was that it was difficult to pronounce my real name, Serijke. The nickname has stuck with me until today and people who care for me still call me Siekie. I love my nickname and when I think about how I got it, I feel that it was given to me by people who helped and really cared for me when I needed it the most in my life. They made me feel safe; we all came from the surrounding community and had all grown up on farms.

I had to change schools in grade 2 (Sub B) because my first school did not support my needs. My parents said that I needed a better education as we were in the apartheid era and they felt that black people were taking over the school. At that time black and white people were not allowed to mix in schools and different race groups attended separate schools. The Department of Education said that the experience and knowledge of the teachers at the school was not up to the required standard.

The new school was a combined primary and secondary school; my mom explained it to me as being a 'Big' school. You would probably think it unlikely when I tell you that I still dream about that hostel and school. I can remember clearly how I felt when I had to go and pick my bed in the hostel dormitory. There were not many beds left and the girls who had been to grade 1 together in this school, were all sleeping next to each other. I got a bed by the door right at the end of the room with no cupboard. They had to make space for a steel cupboard for my use in an already overcrowded room.

My mom made my bed and tried to help me settle in on my first day in the new hostel. Then one of the other children's mothers commented on my bedding. She said in a disgusted tone of voice, 'I don't like the smell of moth balls'. I could see my mother hanging her head in shame. I was embarrassed and felt so sorry for my mom who I could see really wanted to say something. She didn't though and if there is one thing I learnt about my mom, it was that she never interfered in my school or hostel challenges. I had to stand on my own feet and sort things out myself, I had to fight my own battles. Although I knew my mom had used the moth balls so that moths wouldn't eat holes in my bedding, those words, 'I hate the smell of moth balls', stuck in my head for many years. The girls used to tease me and call me 'moth ball girl'. It was a horrible time in my life.

I made one friend who was really special to me. We used to do everything together and had so much fun. It was just the two of us every day, battling through grade 2. We tried to stay out of the way of the girls who teased us relentlessly about so many things; our clothes were too old, our shoes were not branded, our bedding wasn't up to standard. It was a tough time for us.

My gran gave me a camera for a Christmas present. It was purple and worked with a film so you had to ensure that you took the picture correctly the first time otherwise when you had the photos developed, you would pay for 'blurry' pictures. We had great fun taking silly pictures.

I remember how I longed for Fridays as I would become very homesick. Every Friday the big bus would park in front of the hostel and all the kids who travelled to my home town would get onto the bus. Most of the time I sat alone on the ride home. Although my brother went to the same school, he carried on with his life and his friends. He was a popular boy, good at rugby, a great athlete and a real charmer with the ladies. The trip home was an hour long and I tried to sleep most of the time because then time would pass more quickly. I used to sleep when I wanted time to go faster. When I woke up on weekdays in the hostel and realised that it was not Friday, I would feel sad.

On Friday afternoon's, when I woke to the sensation of the bus slowing down to take the turn into town, I was always excited. I used to make the most of my weekends. My brother and I often played as we had when we were still at home. The only difference was that our games were now cricket, rugby and soccer. It was then that I learnt ball sense as we would play for hours. I learnt how to bat and to bowl, I learnt how to kick and to catch a rugby ball. I never learnt how to side step, as I was never quick on my feet. The muscular dystrophy caused me to be slow on my feet.

My brother tackled me every time I had the ball. I think I scored two tries in my entire childhood rugby career and he used to win by 100 points. If my brother got angry with me for not doing as he told me to do, he would tackle me and stick my head in dog poo. To him this was very funny but for me it was no fun at all. But I never gave up and never stopped playing. I always wanted to become better and play harder.

Later on in my school career, I made more friends. The skills that my brother taught me over the weekends at home, I would then teach my friends during the long weeks at school. We were eight girls sharing a dormitory. I taught them how to be tough and how to play rugby. We played rugby and tackled each other regularly. This was fun for me, but something of a drag to them as they were so much faster than I was. It was always hard for me to catch them but I never stopped playing or at least trying to catch them. Even with being slow and disabled, I gave it my all.

My friends tried to teach me to rollerblade but that didn't work out. I had no sense of balance and my ankles would feel as if they were going to break off. I decided to rather get a skateboard and they pushed me around on the skateboard while I sat on it and steered.

One day a friend went around a corner on her rollerblades too quickly and collided with the corner of the window sill. She had a huge hole in her head and there was blood everywhere. I realised then how sensitive I was to blood as I almost fainted at the sight of all that blood.

I loved my skateboard as with it I could at least try and be part of the normal kids' activities. If I wasn't able to do something, I would always find an alternative way to be part of the fun.

When I was seven years old, my brother taught me how to ride a motorcycle. Being too short to get onto the bike, I improvised. I would run next to the bike and jump onto it while it was in motion. Stopping was the hard part as I had to jump off it when I wanted to stop. I had some hard falls and was often battered and bruised as a result. But undeterred, I would get up, brush the dust off, pick up the heavy motorcycle, start it, run next to it and jump on once again. I continued until I mastered the ability of riding the bike without falling.

My brother was a real daredevil on a motorcycle yet he never had any serious accidents. We did, however, mess up my dad's motorbikes, the clutch and front brake levers were always bent as a result of our antics. I had my own bike which was named 'Rooikat.' My dad built our bikes from scratch as he was, and still is, gifted mechanically.

Farmers have to be multi-skilled and my dad was a plumber, an electrician, a builder, a veterinarian and a mechanic. Among many other skills, he taught me how to braai, a very useful skill to have in South Africa. My dad taught me how to ride a horse, although I was never a big horse rider as horses used to scare me. They never listened to me and when I wanted them to go left, they would invariably turn right. We had one horse on the farm named 'Kanon'. He was old, placid and very slow so was a perfect ride for all the kids who came to the farm. One day he accidently threw my cousin off his back. She was very small so didn't fit properly into the saddle and, as Kanon moved forward a little faster than normal, she went flying over his head. Fortunately there were no serious consequences, she just had a little headache and we all had a big scare.

My bedroom was my favourite space on our farm. I used to decorate it with pictures of my sporting heroes and magazine cut outs. All the pictures were glued onto the wall and my dad hated it when we did that. When you removed the pictures, oily marks would be left behind. When you wanted to paint the walls, you first had to wash the oily marks off with sugar soap, which took hours to do. My parents allowed us to do whatever we wanted with our bedrooms and we could choose to paint them any colour we liked. This was my personal space and I loved spending hours in my room as I became older.

Along with the posters came an interest in music. My brother and parents introduced me to different music genres and artists, Bruce Springsteen, Bonnie Tyler, Michael Bolton, Steve Hofmeyer and many others. My dad had an entire box filled with great tape recordings; some he had recorded himself and others were purchased. It made no sense to my brother and me to listen to the same music over and over again so we would steal my dad's tapes and record our own music from the radio over his. This drove my poor dad crazy!

Every time Dad put his Bruce Springsteen tape into the tape deck to listen to, he would get some recording my brother and I had made off the radio. We ruined his entire collection and after a while he had none of his own music left. Not intentionally or maliciously though, we just didn't know any better. We had no CDs, MP3 players or memory cards at that time, only tapes and the radio. My mother had records of music of the sixties and seventies but those were safe from us as there was no way you could make recordings over a record.

On weekends my mom would make us our favourite foods and I used to eat as much as I could. As Mondays drew closer, I would get fearful and anxious. I never told my mom how much I hated school and the hostel as I wanted my parents to be proud of me for being so strong. On Sunday nights my mom would make sure that we washed our hair properly and would also cut our toe nails. I felt so special when she cut my toe nails and spent quality time with us to get us ready for school. We really relished the love and care she showed us. To be honest, I still get my toe nails and nails done by a person who cares for and loves me very much.

Monday mornings meant getting up very early for our journey back to school, a journey that felt long and dreadful to me. In winter Mom would dress us up so warmly that it was almost impossible to move. I'd have so many clothes on that I would start to sweat in the middle of the winter. It was her way of making sure that we didn't get sick and I definitely did not want to get sick. If one of us did get sick, she would make us wear a Vicks menthol block on our chest, attached to our vest. It would make you smell of Vicks rub the whole day and other kids teased you and didn't want to come close to you. I didn't care much about what they thought; if my nose was blocked, the Vicks kept it open and made it possible to breathe properly.

My mom used to make us lunch boxes for break on Mondays, which would include a sandwich made with meat from our Sunday lunch. I was also mocked by the kids about my food, they would say it smelt bad or that my bread looked like vomit. I would go and sit far away from everyone and eat my food alone. I didn't care what they said; my mom had made my lunch for me and I loved it.

The greater part of my first two years in the new school was horrible. When did that change? There was a definite change when I started playing netball, when I became part of a team and we started winning games. I became part of something that changed my life and I was selected to play in the A team, a really good team. Because I was tall and had great ball sense, I was the shooter, the player who has to throw the ball through the hoop to score goals. All through the province I became known as 'the tall girl who could throw a ball through a hoop from a distance'. And also as 'the girl who walked funny'. I was in a group of friends and we started becoming the 'popular' group. The teasing finally stopped, which was a great blessing to me. We spent hours practising netball, tennis and athletics and if we were not doing that we would play at the hostel. When we played hopscotch, I started losing really badly as I did not have any explosive power. When I ran, it looked as if I had pain in my legs or that my muscles were very stiff.

Life was tough in the hostel but you adapted and spent time with people who cared for you. The hostel food was not the best; the eggs were blue most of the time because of the way in which they were prepared. They would put oil into a deep frying pan, break the eggs into the oil and when it popped up, the egg was ready. When they wanted to save a little cost on eggs, they would mix sweetcorn or sausages into the eggs. Breakfast was at 07h00, lunch at 13h00 and dinner at 17h00, so there was a long wait between dinner and breakfast the next morning.

If your mom didn't pack you any tuck, you would have nothing to eat between those times. And if you didn't get pocket money, you were screwed. I can remember one girl who didn't have a lot of money and whose parents lived very far away so she didn't have the privilege of going home every weekend as I did. One morning after breakfast she threw up all her food in the bathroom. The hostel supervisor told her to clean her own vomit up and I saw how she ate the sausages that she had thrown up again. This is just an example of the extreme measures that some kids took to survive.

I got R2 pocket money every week and on Tuesday afternoons we had the opportunity to walk into town. With my R2 I could buy a Vetkoek, cold drink and a packet of chips and still have money left for Chappies bubble gum. My gran would come and visit us once a week and she would bring my brother and me each a packet of tomato flavoured chips, a cream soda drink and a chocolate. I loved Gran and remember how when I got into her car, I would open the cubby hole and help myself to the mints she always kept in there.

She remains one of my role models and taught me all about patience and how to care for family. Before she died, she was permanently on oxygen and struggled to walk. I don't think that I want to get to be that old as it is really sad to see someone so powerful and determined become so frail and vulnerable

She used to visit us on the farm on Sundays and always helped me with my homework. Gran had been a teacher and my late granddad a school principal. She also knitted jerseys for our whole family and made sure that no one ever got cold. At family gatherings, we would all wear the jerseys she had made for us. She also made sure that I had bed socks and scarves for school; I still have some of those scarves today. Whenever I needed money or wanted branded clothes, she would help. Gran helped me through school and university and never said no to me. When I wanted to go home, she would offer her car to my mother so that she could fetch me from boarding school. She never complained about anything, she was humble and loving and I really miss her.

One school holiday when I was 11 years old, I went home and my dad and I went for a ride on the motorbikes to see if everything on the farm was in order. When we were heading back home, he saw that I was changing gears using my heel. Being confused at this, he asked me to walk on my heels.

'I've never been able to walk on my heels, Daddy,' I responded.

'Do you think it is normal not to walk on your heels?' he replied.

'I have never thought about walking on my heels before. I didn't think that it was relevant. Why would a person want to walk on their heels?'

'Because that is normal,' he replied.

I was stunned by his response and just stared at him. I didn't know how to respond. I felt confused. Was I really abnormal?

My cousin came to visit us on the farm that holiday and we had great fun. I can remember us building a raft which unfortunately only made it to the banks of the dam. We used two 20litre drums with open sides and used bags of salt to cover the open ends. We planned to use sticks as oars but as I said, we never made it onto the dam. The drums sank as we lowered them into the water.

My dad had warned us to stay away from the dam and the drums saying that it was dangerous and we could drown. 'We can swim,' we retorted. Sias then came up with the idea that we should cut the drums in half and put them in the water like a boat. We tried that and it worked! My brother joined us on our dam racing, drum paddling expedition. We would make a course on the dam and would race the course to see who was the fastest. That became boring after a while though.

Then we decided that we should all get into the drum to see if it would hold us. It didn't work. As my brother and cousin sat down in the drum, it sank. My brother jumped out and cut his leg badly on the side of the drum. There was blood everywhere, lots of blood. At the sight of the blood I again went pale and fainted. When I came around, I told him that we must go tell my dad that there had been an accident but we left it there when he said that Dad would not be happy as the accident had happened on the dam.

Two days later Sias could hardly walk on the injured leg and it was obvious that the wound should have been stitched. It had now become septic so I had to tell my dad about the accident. Understandably, he was furious. Not because of what had happened but because we hadn't told him about the wound.

'Now we have to do damage control,' he said

We took my brother to the doctor and after a course of antibiotics and a rabies injection, he recovered in a few weeks. Lesson learnt – do not hide things from your parents, no matter how bad they are. Your parents love you and they will be angry but the reason for their anger is that they care for you.

That didn't stop us with our inventions though and we next made a zip line. Not very high but high enough to get the zip line effect. We used ski rope as a wire and tested the elasticity and strength of the rope a few times. All seemed in place and safe.

We realised that we couldn't go down the line with our bare hands so decided that a plastic bag would be ideal as it had nice handles that we could hold onto. My cousin told me to go first.

'Ladies first,' he declared. I have never fallen as hard as I did that day! All I remember is waking up with my cousin standing over me, throwing water onto my face and slapping me. I was lying there like a dead person in the movies, one leg bent behind my neck and one arm twisted into an abnormal position. My entire body was in pain and I thought I had broken my back. But I got up.

My body was stiff for an entire week after that fall. When my mom asked why I was walking as if I'd swallowed a stick, I replied that I was working on a new body posture. We were adventurers who tried weird and wonderful things. We knew what things were supposed to look like but did not have the knowledge of how to go about building them properly. That is what made it so interesting. With lots of injuries in the process, we discovered what did and didn't work. We were curious and it is really important to kill all the critics in your head. Don't be scared to try and do things.

I still have that curiosity. I'm very innovative and will make mistakes but will keep trying until I succeed. I do believe that people are too scared to be curious; they are scared of the unknown because they don't know what will happen or what the consequences will be. Instead of trying, they don't even attempt it at all. If you don't fail many times, you will never gain the knowledge.

Replace your fear with curiosity.

To be curious is to go slowly in order to be able to go fast. You do not have to rush everything. Sometimes it is good to go slowly and to complete a task properly. Doing it quickly might lead to you doing something incorrectly and you will then have to redo the task. By redoing a task, you waste time and wasting time results in you slowing a project down. Then you could miss a deadline.

Answers don't change the world, questions do. How many questions does a four year-old child ask? Why do they ask so many questions?

Because they want to learn and understand how things work.

My cousin would come and visit us every holiday and it was great to have another friend on the farm. We were very naughty and he still recalls the day he tripped me in the hall way. I fell on both my knees and started crying because I had carpet burns on my knees. The more he tried to get me to keep quiet, the harder I cried. My dad sorted him out that day so that he never again tripped me. Growing up among boys made me tough and I could handle more pain than any other girl I knew. My brother said that being tough would come in handy one day and that them being hard on me would only make me a stronger person.

One day we played cricket and I can't remember the reason my brother got angry at me but he threw the cricket ball at me. It hit me on my right hand so hard that a small bone in my hand broke, on impact. The bump of that broken bone is still on my hand. I wasn't allowed to cry, because 'only sissies cry'. My brother and his friends would tease me if I cried so I never went to the doctor or told my mom about my hand. My brother said that if I told my mom, I would never be allowed to play with them again. I wanted to show them that I was not a softie and that I could handle the boys.

The key is to view everything as an opportunity to make your life better. That's how ultra-successful people are hardwired. Be relentless and never give up.

Be fascinated by your own ignorance…remember that your brain decides how long a moment lasts. Make every moment in your life a memorable one.

Painful

One winter evening, I ran out of the hostel dining room, ready to go and play. It was already dark outside and I didn't see the bone a dog had dropped on the floor. I stepped onto the star shaped point of the bone and immediately collapsed from the pain. There was blood everywhere and you all know by now that I faint when I see blood. So just imagine how I reacted to my own blood. For me it came close to being a near-death experience.
My parents were informed about the accident but they were told that everything was in order. They were told my foot would be bandaged and I would be given painkillers. I can remember that day like yesterday and I couldn't sleep a wink that night as the pain was so excruciating I wanted to cut my foot off because of it. I wanted my mom, I wanted to go home. According to the hostel nurse I was fine and just wanted a little attention.

After two days of this excruciating pain, I pulled myself out of the bed. I couldn't stand on my foot which was as big as a soccer ball by that stage. There were red marks running along my legs. I crawled to the pay phone where I made a collect call to my parents as I did not have any money. When my mom answered, I just cried and cried. I told her that she must come and fetch me otherwise I would cut my foot off. It wasn't long before my dad walked into my room and I cried and cried some more. Dad was in shock when he saw me. He took me home and immediately make an appointment with the doctor in the nearby town.

We went to the doctor on the afternoon of the following day, the only time he had an appointment available for me. It was now four days after I had stood on the bone. When the doctor saw me he didn't waste any time but phoned the hospital that was 170 kilometres away and made an emergency appointment. I had severe blood poisoning.

I heard him telling my dad that we had 45 minutes to get to the hospital as if we did not get there in time they would have to consider amputating my left foot. I remember telling my dad that it was a two hour drive to the City and we would never make it. He said that I should not worry and he would make sure we make it.

We picked my mother up from the farm where she was ready with clothes packed and off we drove to the City. The blue car was going to be tested for its speed. 10 kilometres out of town we were stopped by a traffic cop but when Dad explained the situation to him, he let us go. The cop was very nice and informed other traffic cops on the route about our situation. So we were not pulled over again on our way to hospital. We didn't make it in 45 minutes but we did get there very quickly.

I told my parents that I really didn't want to lose my foot as then I wouldn't be able to play netball again. And if I didn't play netball, the kids would start teasing me again. That was the first time I told my mom that I used to get teased.

In the hospital I had to put on light blue theatre clothes. I can remember that the underwear they gave me was way too big. My mom told me just to leave it off as underwear was the least of my problems at that moment. I was pushed into the operating room for the emergency operation and I can still picture my mother's face when I went through the door; she was crying and looked so worried. I don't remember how long the operation lasted but remember waking up in the hospital. The doctor came to see how I was doing and showed me the bone they had removed from my foot. He showed me where the bone had entered my foot and how it had broken off next to my little toe. Then he explained that if we cleaned the wound exactly as we would be told to, I would be able to keep my foot.

I was happy but didn't know what I was letting myself in for. The first time they cleaned my foot in the hospital, I realised that the healing process was going to be a long one and I would need to be strong. They opened the wound and pulled out cotton wool that had been packed into it to stop the bleeding. The pus that came out filled up three kidney bowls. After the draining, they injected fluid into the wound with a syringe as long as my pinkie finger. It was the most painful thing I had ever experienced! They then forced a new piece of cotton wool back into the hole to prevent bleeding. I thought that it was only this one time that the procedure had to be done but I was horribly wrong. The next day the nurse came and told us to watch and listen closely to what she was doing. If we cleaned the wound every day, I could go home instead of having to stay in hospital for a week.

My mom and I thought that this would be an easy task but the first night we did it on our own, I fainted again. I couldn't handle the syringe needle. The second night I fainted again from watching the pus draining from the wound. And so it continued. For a whole week I fainted every night when my mom cleaned the wound. But every day the pain became less and the swelling started to go down. My left foot still has the hole where the bone entered it. This was the first of many painful experiences that I have had to endure during my life. I received a card and chocolate bouclé from my cousin and his card read, 'I'm so glad you didn't die. I love you and want you to get better soon'. After a long recovery process I did recover fully but, through this experience I realised that anything in life can be deadly, even a chewed bone.

Surviving

I went back to school after I had recovered and it was initially hard to play netball again. My foot felt stiff and I had become really unfit. I didn't give up but instead started training really hard and got myself back to full fitness. I also started swimming again. I did well at swimming but didn't like it as much because it wasn't a team sport and I found it boring. I broke my first swimming record in grade 3, the 50 metre backstroke. I achieved many first places in swimming and my mom thought that I would become a professional swimmer.

My gran thought that I would become a professional athlete because I came first in the 100 metre dash when I was in grade 1. However, I was the only child running the race. As funny as it may sound, Gran had high hopes and dreams for me. She always believed that I would become great.

I started throwing the javelin at the age of 10 and had to compete in an older age category as the sport only started from 12 years and older. I placed first in the first competition that I participated in. I also did well in Shot Put in primary school but continued the javelin throw until I was 18 as I loved the sport. I used to travel to the City to compete in bigger competitions. I tried out everything that my body allowed me to.

The race I remember most clearly is the first time I ran the 1 200meters. I had trained hard for the race and my dad gave me an energy drink before the race. I drank a bit too much of it and was on a sugar high. So the race started off well but when I began the last lap, I realised that everyone else had already finished the race and I was the only one still running. The people who had run with me were standing next to the track enjoying water. I refused to give up and although it was very embarrassing, I finished the race. Then I fell flat on my face on the grass. In my entire life I had never before been so tired.

While I was lying on my face, I didn't want to get up and it felt as if the entire world was laughing at me. When I did stand up, nobody except my brother was laughing and he didn't speak to me for the rest of the day. He is very competitive and hates it when I lose. He taught me that if you give your best, you will win. Only losers say that they've *tried* their best.

I love thinking like a champion. Sias was a great role model to me on the sports field and was the best at everything he did. He was born with natural talent and seldom came second at anything. He did not waste any of that talent when he was young.

Use exercise as an elite achievement tool. Daily exercise fuels passion, beats stress and accelerates focus. Use it to win. Behave like the person you want to become. Eventually you will convince your mind to think like that person. I wanted to be as good as my brother, to be great at everything I did.

It was after that race that I became suspicious of my abilities as something just didn't feel right. I didn't say anything about it and continued with my life. As the end of the year approached, it was time for class photos. I was stunned when we received our individual photos as my teeth looked as if I was meant to be in a horror movie. I asked my parents if there was anything we could do about this 'horrible teeth situation'. My parents took me to a dentist in the City who referred me to an orthodontist. That was the first day of four and a half years of wearing braces. 'Lovely,' I thought, 'now they are going to tease me again.'

Luckily I wasn't the only one with braces at that stage as there were a few kids at school who also had braces. It actually became a very popular thing among the kids but was also painful and hard to have braces in the hostel. I had to wear a harness that went around my neck and then clipped onto my teeth and made me look like a horse. 'All of this to have beautiful teeth,' I thought to myself. After the horse-brace, I moved on to wearing elastic bands. These small elastics were supposed to pull your teeth into the correct position. Recently I had a dream about those elastics and in my dream I forgot to replace them. The elastics started to rot and my teeth started falling out. It was more a nightmare than a dream!

I couldn't believe that 25 years after my braces were removed, I dreamt about having them again. Every time you wanted to eat something, you had to remove the elastics. My mom was always picking up elastics everywhere. It was such a mission, and I used to leave them on my plate after I had eaten. To everybody around me this was disgusting; to me it was my normal.

You couldn't bite an apple but first had to cut it into small pieces and then eat those. I know that my braces broke a few times. Once it was when I had 'droewors' and another time was when I teased one of my friends and she accidently hit me on my mouth with a broom. As it broke, the wire got stuck into my lip. I had to phone my parents to come and fetch me to take me to the dentist who was two hours away. Another painful incident!

The older we got, the smaller our hostel rooms became. The last room I remember in primary school was shared with three other girls. The four of us were good friends, my life was good and we planned to stay in the same school until we finished grade 12. At that stage we became interested in boys and we all had boyfriends. You never spoke to your boyfriend; you would only write letters to each other and buy them chocolates or something. It really wasn't very romantic. One of my friends used to have more than one boyfriend at a time, I don't know how she did it but she managed to master the skill. We would also draw pictures or hearts for our boyfriends and I used to draw palm trees or flowers. I would also write, 'I like you' in every letter. I was in love every time I got a new boyfriend but it never lasted for longer than two weeks. My brother told me a while ago that he once caught me holding hands with a guy while we were watching a movie in the joint TV Room in the hostel. He was much older than I was and we were holding hands under a blanket. We were so shy and innocent then and I was so embarrassed that I never spoke to the guy again.

Children's innocence can become their biggest fear. Allow your children to explore and experience things the way they see them as no two brains are alike. You are never too old to explore, experience adventure or just do things differently.

Chapter Four

Make a Choice

Confused, scared and not knowing what to expect from life was how I felt after having been diagnosed with muscular dystrophy. My parents did everything in their power to reassure me, although I think they were even more scared than I was. They knew that we had to do something, so they started doing research to try and inform them and get some answers to all the questions we had about the condition.

There was a great deal of discussion going on after our return from the foot specialist. One of the topics was getting more information about my condition and another current topic was the release of Nelson Mandela from prison. At that stage I had no idea who Mr Nelson Mandela was. All I knew was that he had been in jail for a very long time and that he was going to set the 'black people' free. I was young and I didn't have much of an idea of what was happening in the world. I did know that no black people were allowed to attend our school but I didn't understand why that was, especially as my best friends on the farm were the children of our black workers. I always wanted to take my friends from the farm with me to school but my parents told me that was not allowed. I can remember that public bathrooms had notices outside reading 'whites only' and that even the benches in the railway stations had the same notices on them. There are many other things relative to the apartheid era that I can remember but my book is not about politics, it's about life.

There was much speculation and people would go around saying that all the whites are going to be killed on the day Nelson Mandela was released. We all know that didn't happen and that everything just got better and better in our country, with regard to equality. What really did get out of hand was the number of farm killings and the amount of protection the people were getting from the police. The government put an end to the local commandoes run by the farmers and they were no longer allowed to have commandoes. Security on the farms just decreased and many attacks on farmers around us took place. People who we knew very well were murdered and the scary thing is that this situation is only getting worse. South Africa's economy is very dependent on its farmers so this is a matter of great concern.

The stories were told from farmhouse to farmhouse. One day a farmer came in from the field and found his whole family skinned and hanged on ropes on their porch. Imagine coming home and finding your family murdered in that way? There was another murder where the farmer, his wife and daughter were attacked. The farmer was forced to watch how 'they' raped his wife and daughter. His eyes were forced open and he was told that they would all be killed if he did not watch. The attackers killed the wife and daughter anyway but did not kill the farmer, the killers left him alive to feel the pain of losing his family. He later committed suicide as he couldn't handle the trauma of that day.

I grew up in the years when the country was transitioning from apartheid to democracy. In 1990, the year Mandela was released, I was starting my grade 7 year. According to the Department of Education, we would have to leave our current small school and move to one in the city as the standard of education would go down.

The politics of the time were not the only reason why I had to move schools for the third time. I had to get the necessary medical care and do rehabilitation exercises with a biokineticist and only one school could accommodate and care for me at that time. I needed transport every second day to go to the hospital for my rehabilitation exercises. My parents were not able to take me because they lived out of town on the farm.

We were making milkshakes in our massive farm kitchen on a warm summer's day when my dad told us that we had to choose new schools. My brother and I didn't want to be separated so we wanted to go to the same school again. I wanted his support and guidance, I needed my role model. Sias suggested the farmer's school in the North West province. The school would work for him because he wanted to become a farmer. I would also have loved to go to that school but would have to go to a school in the City in order to get the treatment I needed.

We were devastated at the thought of being separated from each other for the remainder of our school careers. The only thing that kept us going was looking forward to Fridays and school holidays. It's the circle of life... On Mondays you started wishing for Friday to arrive. On Sunday you felt nauseous when you started packing your bags to go back to boarding school. It was terrible and heart breaking for us most of the time. Believe me when I say that life was getting harder and harder. 'When is the change going to end, when will I ever feel that this life is a good place?' I used to wonder. It felt as if that day would never come. I started to move away from God and neglected my spirituality. I started questioning God more and more.

Little did I know that everything happening in my life would be lessons that I learnt from. All those lessons helped me both to become confident and to develop a positive self-image which made me believe in myself. It made me realise that everything is possible through the strength that God gives me on my journey through life.

Some of my friends who were at school with me in the small town, were also changing schools and most of them were going to the same school that I was. I was glad that we would all be together again.

When I received the brochure for the new school and saw the rules and regulations of the boarding school, I decided that I didn't want to go there anymore. I was frightened as I had a fear of wearing dresses. Growing up on a farm, I was most accustomed to wearing shorts and a T-shirt and to walking barefoot. The rules stated that we had to wear dresses at all times and that shorts and T-shirts were not allowed. I did not have one dress in my cupboard. We were also not allowed to wear flip flops but instead had to wear sandals. I did not like the sound of their dress code at all!

My bags were packed and we were ready for the road trip. We were going via the city first, where my parents would drop me off and then go on to my brother's new school. I felt a little bit of excitement as my new journey was starting, with new adventures, new teachers and the city. I had no idea what to expect of the city, having lived on the farm for 12 years and only having attended school in a small town. The town consisted of a post office, a co-op, a café and a bank. The local café sold Russian sausages or fish and chips. That is what I was used to and what I knew. Now I was going to this big city with its big buildings and take-away restaurants. You probably wouldn't believe that I did not know what a pizza was. On the occasions when we had gone to the city, we usually ate sandwiches or fried chicken.

Small towns like ours did not have traffic lights, only stop streets. And no one ever stopped at the stop streets anyway.

Nevertheless, I was ready for this challenge. I needed to accept the fact that this was going to be my new life and that I had to make a decision to accept it. I can still smell the 'blue rain flowers' that were blooming in front of the hostel when we arrived at our destination in the city. Every time I smell that scent, I remember the day I was dropped in what felt like the middle of nowhere. The building was much bigger than the other two hostels that I had lived in had been. They allocated me to a room and I learnt I was sharing with a girl who I knew from my previous school. I was relieved to know that I would not be sharing with a stranger. I got lost walking to my room more than once; it just felt far too big to me. I did not know where I was going and what to do when I got there, I did not know where the dining room was. I did not know anything and felt completely out of place!

There were many staircases and long, cold hallways in the hostel. You could hear your voice echo when you spoke in those hallways. My mom helped me to unpack my bags. I had made sure this time that my bedding did not smell of moth balls. I had a blue duvet cover with pink flowers on it. After my bags were unpacked it was time to say goodbye to my brother and my parents. Dad was wearing a white pair of pants and Mom smelt as good as she always did. Sias was wearing his new school uniform and his hair was neatly cut to perfection. I started crying and I didn't want to let go of my dad. I was holding him tightly and I asked him not to leave me alone. He took a handkerchief from his pocket and used it to wipe my tears away. I kept that handkerchief for months afterwards because it smelled like my dad. Although it was no longer very clean after a month or three, I would still use it to wipe my tears away when I cried. Some days were much better than others and I discovered that it was important to keep busy. Most of the time, however, I felt sick to my stomach from missing my family.

I remember that I kept myself busy by watching TV a great deal of the time during my grade 7 year. I ate a lot and did very little training for sports. I had played netball for the under 11 team which won the district trophy in the year I played for them in my previous school. At the netball trials in my new school, I only made it into the fifth team. I felt that was not worthwhile so I did not go to practises. I didn't feel it was worth playing unless I played in the first or second team. At the same time, I was not motivated and did not have the willpower to practice to become better or to work harder at making the first team. I felt that I'd rather become fat and lazy and waste my precious energy on doing nothing. My homework suffered too as I did not bother to do much of it. My days consisted of going to school, doing my rehab exercises three times a week and watching TV. My friends were very active and tried to encourage me to go and play netball and tennis. I would only last for one session and then I would not go back again.

The doctor told me that I was not allowed to play any contact sport because if I injured my ankles or knees, the injury would take months to heal and it might even never heal fully. I didn't want to risk getting any injuries as I didn't want to do anything that could result in me having to use a wheelchair for the rest of my life. I was in a place where I wanted nothing in life and I didn't want to do anything about that situation. Life turned its back on me, so I turned my back on the world. I felt useless, was getting really fat and also eating very unhealthily. At that stage of my life I didn't really understand what healthy eating and a healthy lifestyle were. To me eating was only a matter of survival, my main concern was to be careful of doing anything that could lead to an injury.

One day a group of us were sitting around in the hostel, feeling very bored. We put the plug into the bathtub and ran the water so that the bath overflowed. We then took washing powder and sprinkled it over the wet floor. The bathrooms were big and had slippery tile floors. We would run from one side of the bathroom and ski to the other side. The more foam, the more fun we had. We took turns and were having great fun. There was foam everywhere! One of the twins was standing next to me when another friend asked her why blood was running down her leg. When she looked down, she saw that there was a large piece of flesh ripped out of her bum and blood from it was streaming down her leg. As you readers know by now, I obviously almost fainted when I saw all the blood. This time, however, I only went pale but did not faint. I helped to get her onto the back of one of my friends and she was then carried down six flights of stairs and all the way to the hostel supervisor.

She had ripped her leg open on a screw on the back of the bathroom door. When we had started our game, there had been a rubber doorstop on the screw but one of us must have bumped it off by accident while we were sliding. The head of the hostel had the injured twin taken to hospital and she came back that evening with stiches in her wound. She had needed a few stitches and was in pain. That was the first and last time we played the sliding in washing powder game!

I did not go home as much as I had before. Although my parents did try to get me home every weekend, it was not always possible. On some weekends, I went to visit my uncle and aunt so as not to be the only kid left in the hostel. A big hostel can be a very scary place when you are there alone. One day after lunch I was running to the TV room as I was in a hurry to watch my afternoon TV programmes. I wasn't watching where I was going and slipped and fell on the stairs. As I rolled down the stairs, my ankle hit the side rails and my head the stairs. After tumbling down about six steps, my body came to an abrupt stop. I was in tremendous pain with my foot hurting the most. I thought to myself that this was it and, because of the pain, thought I must have torn my ligaments. My ankle had swollen and instantly turned blue. 'I'm in trouble now,' I thought.

I was taken to hospital where the examining doctor confirmed that I had torn all three of my ligaments as well as breaking a bone in my foot. He said that it would be impossible to put my foot in a cast because I would lose too much muscle strength if they put it into a cast for six weeks. I would have to wear a foot brace and walk on crutches instead and I needed intensive physiotherapy for six to eight weeks to help the foot recover. That was the longest eight weeks of my life! Walking on crutches was no joke and my hands were constantly bruised. They also blistered and my shoulders became inflamed. I stayed on the third floor of the hostel and had to climb five flights of stairs to get to my room; it took me 30 minutes. I got really depressed and lonely at that time. My friends carried on with their lives, played sport and kept busy with the things they enjoyed. It took me 10 weeks to fully recover from my fall.

My ligaments healed perfectly and my doctors and I were very surprised when we realised that I had recovered fully. The only part that was still sensitive was the broken bone which also healed but remained painful. I realised then that if I was going to sit around all day doing nothing, nothing would happen. Being constantly scared that I might break or tear something, would only lead to me living in fear of the 'what if' every day of my life. I was really pitying myself and

I realised that I could fall down the stairs at any time. So why not take the risk and start playing sport again?

What could be the worst that could happen? I'd already broken a bone and torn three ligaments while trying to be careful. My group of friends always invited me to go and play hockey with them after dinner but I always said no because I wasn't allowed to run. Without being able to run, you can't very well do much sport. On the school athletics day, I would sit in the pavilion like a loser, not doing anything. That year had many challenges and passed slowly but surely. I grew quiet and distant.

I missed home tremendously and always longed to go home to see my brother and to be with my parents. When I did get home on weekends, however, it was also not as much fun anymore as my dad had started drinking a lot.

Alcohol was and still is a problem in my family. My granddad, great-granddad and great-great granddad were all heavy drinkers. This was a part of my life that I did not want to remember or dwell on.

We always made sure that we went to bed early. I've never spoken much about the alcohol problem in my family as I felt that it was a very private matter and I didn't want anyone to know what was really going on at home. It wasn't easy for my mum who protected us most of the time.

If I had to write about every single thing that happened at that time, my book would be all about alcohol and how it almost destroyed my family and my own life.

I want to acknowledge my dad for having the strength to stop his drinking problem. Although I did not know him for 25 years, I started to get to know him in the last 10 years for who he really is. He is a loving father that went through a time in his life where he lost control. He tried to keep our family together in a time where it was really hard in the farming industry. He taught me how to control my temper and how to appreciate life. Many people have asked me why I still live in the same town all these years. The answer is simple, for the first time in 30 years I have my family around me. My parents and brother can visit at any time. When I miss them, I can visit them, I thought I knew them then, but now I really see them for who they are. My family are strong, hardworking and respectful people. They have grid and self-respect. I want to acknowledge my mother for staying with my dad during the tough times. She is a true example of obeying her wedding vows – in sickness and in health. I am grateful and blessed that they never got divorced after all the drama they went through. They are an inspiration to me.

Chapter Five

History Creates Values

The school had many traditions and one was that on the school's birthday, the whole school would go to the Women's War Monument to honour the women and children who died in the Anglo Boer War. 26 370 women and children died during that war, many of them in concentration camps.

The Women's Memorial

During the darkest days of the war, the idea of immortalising the selfless love of women and children for posterity in the form of a memorial, occurred to President Steyn. Immediately after the end of the war, a serious illness forced him to go to Europe for medical treatment but he did not lose sight of his dream. On his return to his farm, *Onze Rust*, in March 1905, one of his first actions was to take steps to realise this long-cherished ambition. Because this was considered to be a matter of national importance on which the nation in general should be consulted, it was decided to call a conference of all the Dutch Reformed churches and political organisations in the four colonies. They met in on 7 February 1907 under the chairmanship of President Steyn. At the joint conference it was decided that 'The time has come to erect a monument on South African soil to the glorious memory of the mothers, women and children who, during the recent war, passed away, or had otherwise suffered bitterly, either in the concentration camps or outside.'.

A 'Subscription List for the National Women's Memorial', together with a powerful appeal for contributions by President Steyn from the wealthy as well as from the poor, men, women and children, began circulating shortly after the conference. The amount to be raised in this manner was a substantial one, especially in those times when Afrikaans people were suffering extreme poverty. The money was collected in pennies and shillings; contributions of a pound or more were rare exceptions. Although individual contributions were small, such large numbers of

Afrikaans-speaking, as well as English-speaking and Jewish citizens contributed to the fund that the erection of the memorial soon became a matter of national importance. During the unveiling of the memorial, the president could justly declare, 'The erection of this memorial was made possible not only by the wealth of the wealthy, but especially by the poverty of the poor.'

I still have a passion for history and my school had an interesting history, having been established in 1907 by President Steyn. He wanted to create a school for Afrikaans women, a school which would be a cornerstone for women to become great leaders in their communities. He stated that it was his mission to create higher education for women because he believed they were the future of the country. He wanted the women to have a strong Christian background and the school still has strong Christian values and morals in place.

I studied most of the history of the school and always had a passion for the Anglo Boer War. I had a teacher who became a mentor to me in the field of history. She was very strict and the girls were scared of her. I wasn't scared of her as I liked her and we got along very well. I invited her to our farm one weekend and we went to explore the concentration camps in the area together. She always quoted from the Bible, 'Are two sparrows sold for a farthing? And one of them shall not fall on the ground without your Father knowing. Fear ye not therefore, ye are of more value than many sparrows.'

We had to be young ladies and always had to look impeccable for school and live by the high values that were demonstrated to us. Our school dresses were the colour of pumpkin and we called them 'pumpkin dresses.' We were not allowed to wear short dresses; the hem of your dress had to be exactly three finger spaces above your knee. The girls used to pull their belts down around their buttocks and this was a sure way to irritate our teachers. We were also not allowed to wear gel in our hair or to colour it. Your nails had to be kept short and we were not allowed to wear nail polish.

The teachers used to tell me to stop wearing gel in my hair and I would explain that it was mousse, not gel. As a result of my disability, I battled to find the correct school shoes. Normal school shoes were not comfortable and used to hurt my feet. I asked my parents to write a letter to the headmistress to explain my situation to her. She understood fully and allowed me to wear shoes that were comfortable. In the beginning of secondary school, it was difficult to wear my normal Nike trainers to school. It was against the standards of the school and I looked out of place but I really couldn't care less what the girls said behind my back. As long as my feet where comfortable, I was happy. Prefects and teachers would all stop me and ask why I was wearing the incorrect shoes. At first I would stop and explain the situation politely to them but by the 10th time I got impatient and after that I sent them to speak to the head mistress.

I think that part of my impatient character today started at a very young age as I always wanted to do things that other kids could do. I always wanted to look like the other girls at school did, I always wanted to be able to walk like other people walked. Most people thought that I did what I did to draw attention to myself. And maybe, to some extent, I did; I would wear bright red shoes so that people had a reason to look at the way I walked. I did not only try to be different, I *was* always different.

Initiation

I will never forget the first two weeks of my grade 8 year at high school. One day before the school term started, all the grade 8 pupils had to get together in the school hall. During this session we were introduced to the matric (grade 12) girls and listened to a speech by the head girl, who was very conservative and polite. After that all hell broke loose! There was a girl on the stage who was speaking very loudly and giving instructions on what we had to do. I did not register half the things she said because I was scared of this girl, who seemed very domineering. Each of us had to find a matric girl who would be our 'mother' for the rest of the year. I think I was picked last of all the grade 8s, maybe because I was known as' the girl who walks funny' or 'the girl with the limp'. I was very self-conscious at that age, or should I say throughout my entire high school career. When everyone had matric 'mothers', a tall girl with long blonde hair and a lovely smile approached me. In a sweet voice she asked politely, 'Would you like to be my 'Sot'?' Neither she nor I had much of a choice as we were the last two girls left unpaired. That was the day she named me 'Chicken' but fortunately that name only stuck for two weeks. After that my nickname was again 'Siekie'. The word 'Sot' was given to the entire grade 8 group and it was a name that we went by because we were new to high school. The aim wasn't to belittle or insult anyone, it was just a name they used. In 2009 the school changed the term used to 'Plankie'(this word means 'a small piece of wood'). The head mistress explained that the term was used for all newcomers to the school, 'Because they are still raw wood that needs to be formed into either beautiful wooden furniture or the opposite, which is an ugly tomato case.' I thought that this was a great analogy to use as each girl had the opportunity to decide how she would form her own character. The school gave us the guidelines and knowledge on how to build a great character and also assisted us in developing a great value system. We were allowed to make our own decisions on how to handle the inauguration and begin our high school careers. I learnt that complaining would not solve any of our problems. 'Go with the flow and do what is asked of you. You made the choice to be in this great school. Make the best of it and enjoy every second,' we were advised.

On our first day of high school, we had to wear clothes pegs as hair clips and a dish cloth as a bib. The day was called 'washing day' and you had to look as if you were doing your washing. I must also mention that this was in January, the middle of summer and it was really hot. The more clothes you wore, the hotter you got.

In the evenings all the hostel girls had to assemble on the hockey field and we soon realised that this was definitely not to play hockey. We had to leopard crawl and sneak up on the Hill. You had to be so invisible that the Hill couldn't see you so I lay flat on my stomach with my head slightly lifted off the grass.

'What are you looking at, Sot?' was a yell I got from a grade 12 girl. 'Head down!'

If I had to go down any further, I would have become a mole. The rules were simple; the one who came first would have to do the race again and the one who came last had to start again. Basically, we all had to cross the finish line at exactly the same time and we ended up doing the race three times. Although my knees and elbows were bleeding, it was still a lot of fun. I learnt how to leopard crawl and still remember that today. I also learnt that a mountain has feelings and eyes that can see you. Use your imagination.

After that exercise we had to make a huge circle and for about 15 minutes we walked in a circle doing lunges and flexing our chests. As we did this very painful move, we also had to say the following, 'I must, I must, develop my bust.' After that exercise, I decided that I didn't want breasts any more. I was so stiff the next day that I couldn't even wash my hair in the shower. It was also impossible to climb stairs, not to mention going to the toilet. Everything was hard to do and I mean *everything!*

We had a watermelon fun day with the local boys' school. They would come to our school in a big bus and we would eat watermelons together. Boring! That is obviously not what happened. There were watermelons and there were girls and boys. But the watermelon was not eaten; it was thrown and smeared on one another's bodies. I've never been as sticky as I was that day! As you know by now, I was not that fast but I was clever. I hid under trees and in trees and underneath the pavilion and when the guys passed, I jumped out and threw watermelon at them.

I can also remember that one of our theme days was 'Travel Day'. On that day we had to pack our suitcases and go to school with all the clothes from our cupboards packed. Your bag had to be heavy or you would get two drops of chilli sauce on your tongue. Or you would have to carry someone else's bags as well as your own. Trust me when I say it was hot and heavy duty carrying! Sweat was dripping off my forehead the entire day; the African sun is not for the faint hearted! I smelt like old cooking oil at the end of a school day. It was extremely hard but great fun.

Whenever you thought you had free time, the grade 12 girls would call you to participate in some kind of event or embarrassing move. I'm not sure what one girl did wrong, but when I passed her on the hockey field, she was sitting on a rock as if she was hatching an egg. The grass was freshly cut and she had made a nest from the loose grass and sat on that rock for hours, pretending that it was an egg. I don't believe that the egg ever hatched...

We had to take picnic baskets to school for our grade 12 mothers one day. As boarders it was difficult to get food for a picnic basket but we made plans and got what we needed for our baskets. It was not a very exciting picnic but at least it was something. I was running around on the morning of the picnic day trying to find a flower to pin on my grade 12 mother's school dress. When I finally found a flower that looked pretty in the school garden, it smelt horrible. I picked the flower anyway because it was pretty. I can still picture her face when I gave the flower to her. She said that it was a garlic plant and that she was allergic to garlic. I apologised profusely and luckily she did not mind not having a flower. After all the trouble I had been through to get food for her picnic basket, she did not touch it as she said that she was on a diet. 'What waste of good food,' I thought. So I ate it.

The two weeks of our initiation went by in a flash. It was a time of making fools of ourselves but also of bonding and learning how to have fun.

On the last day of the initiation fortnight, we put on a concert. My friends and I put on *Cinderella*. It was fun, embarrassing and playful all at the same time and our play came together nicely in the end; everyone had a great laugh. We had to eat disgusting porridge that was specially designed for us. It tasted horrible and it burnt like hell. After eating the porridge, you had to swallow aloe water. We had to dress up in our swimming costumes and also wear a black rubbish bag and a swimming cap. This was the only way you were allowed to jump into the swimming pool to cool down your burning mouth. I used a pot of Vaseline on my face to prevent my skin from burning. The Vaseline started melting in the sun and the black rubbish bag was as hot as hell, it felt as if I was in a body sauna. To make matters worse, we had to do the exercise barefoot and there were lots of thorns on the hockey field. It was a real challenge but we all did it together as a team.

Mind over matter! Doing all of these things moulded us into a strong bunch of girls. Our initiation helped build character and created team spirit. If you observe how troops do military training, you can see the determination they have to succeed. This fortnight's initiation taught us girls to be disciplined, to listen and to have respect for people older than ourselves. It showed us that by having fun and living for the moment, you can conquer anything.

My message to parents is, don't be too protective over your children. Your children know that you care about them so allow them to have fun. Allow them to experience pain. Life is not easy, don't make it seem as if it is a rose garden out there in the real world. You can guide your children but allow them to make their own decisions. Whatever their choice is, they need to take responsibility for it. Allow your children to be their own 'normal' as each child is unique.

Chapter Six

Accept Your Normal

At this stage I'm going to go back to a traumatic time in my schooldays as I think this section is relevant here. The incident I am going to recount also played a significant role in me becoming the person I am today so forgive me for jumping around in time.

My friends didn't treat me as if I was different because of my condition, they treated me as their friend and not as some kind of alien. At one stage in my high school years, however, I did feel like an alien as I was rejected by most of my best friends. That was just after I had an operation on my right foot and was wheelchair-bound for six weeks while I recovered.

The operation was performed by the same doctor who had diagnosed my illness and it was done in a hospital in City in the North. I had wanted to have both feet operated on at the same time as I wanted to get the surgery over and done with. I can now really thank the doctor for refusing to do both operations at the same time as if he had, my life would be very different today.

The operation consisted of him breaking all my toes and removing the cartilage from them. He then replaced the cartilage with stainless steel pins about the thickness of an ear bud which were inserted into the tops of my toes, connecting in the centre of my foot. The doctor also wanted to decrease the height of my foot arch in order to make walking easier and to prevent more bunions from forming. He made a 10cm cut under my foot to stretch the ligament which released the tension in the bridge and lowered it; in medical terms these are the foot dorsiflexors/evertors. I am not able to move my feet outwards or upwards; I can only drop them down and move them inwards. I can't move my toes much so no wiggling of toes for me.

When I woke up after the operation I, spoke English fluently; my parents had no idea why this suddenly happened. I was yelling to the nurse to take off my shoes and telling her that my shoes were too tight and were making my feet feel numb. Of course, the shoe I was referring to was the cast on my foot. The more I wanted to remove the cast, the more the nurses would pin me down so that I could not touch it. The next thing I felt was a sharp sting in my buttocks and then I fell asleep again. My mom told me later that I swore a lot in English that day; she couldn't handle it and she and my dad both started crying as it was very difficult for them to see me helpless and in pain. At that stage the doctor couldn't tell whether the operation had been successful and we would only know the results when the cast was removed in six weeks' time.

If I had to effectively describe the pain that I went through, I would have to mostly use profanity! I was on strong pain medication and became constipated and irritable as a result. I had to sleep with my bed on two bricks so that the blood wouldn't flow to my toes as it rather had to flow to my heart. My leg and foot felt dead and the pain was excruciating; if the sheet on my bed so much as touched my toes or the pins, I would start crying in agony. I had thought that I could handle pain but *this* pain was at a different level from anything I'd previously experienced. We had to do ice treatments for weeks after the operation to prevent swelling and I did them diligently for 20 minutes in the morning and 20 in the evening. I don't know what I did wrong, but on day three after the operation, we had to go back to the hospital because it felt as if my little toe was breaking off.

It did almost break off as I'd apparently left the ice treatments on my foot for too long. This resulted in frostbite and my toes turned blue and became ice cold. The muscular dystrophy prevented my nervous system from alerting me to the fact that I was doing something wrong. The doctor then instructed me to do heat treatments for two days and see what happened so that's what we did. But then the stainless steel pins would heat up in my foot and become very uncomfortable. After heat treatment, we would do ice treatment and I then developed 'winter toes'. My toes now became pink and itched like hell and I felt like scratching them continually. The cast felt as if it was too small; definitely not my happiest memory!

After being at home for two weeks, I had to go back to school. I used a wheelchair to get around so I wasn't able to carry my school case. I could do very little for myself and found it extremely frustrating and annoying. I was used to playing hockey, going to the gym or cycling. Sitting still was really no longer my thing and brought back bad memories of my grade 7 school year. I was very conscious of my weight at that time and exercising was the main driver to keeping my weight under control.

I had to be very careful when I moved around and especially had to make sure that no one bumped against my toes. Moving between classes was very difficult as I always had to ask someone to carry my case for me. Sometimes no one felt like carrying it and I would then put the case on my back and move using crutches. There was one person who always supported me by carrying my case and pushing me back to the hostel. It was a steep climb back to the hostel and it was impossible for me to push myself up as I was too weak. What I never expected from her were the stories she went and told behind my back. She told people that I felt sorry for myself and that it was becoming unbearable for her. One day I was waiting for her to push me back to the hostel after school and she never arrived so I guess that was a way of making her feelings known.

That day a girl who I had never thought would do so came to my assistance. When I got back to my room, I found that my roommate had moved out. It was lonely and quiet in my room which was actually the old piano room so it was soundproof. No one came to visit me and depression was lurking on my doorstep. In those days nobody understood what depression was; we all just carried on with our lives. When someone exhibited a personality change, the girls would start gossiping and would reject her because she was becoming 'weird'.

While I was in England for my gap year, the person who rejected me phoned me to apologise and to say that she felt really bad about what she had done. When I got back from England and she got back from America, things were very different from the way they had been at school and we became more than just best friends.

I was wishing the days away and there were many days when I just wanted to cut the irritating cast open and remove it myself. I didn't gain weight because of suffering from depression, which also resulted in a loss of appetite. Finally the day arrived for the cast to be removed... I was sitting on the bed in the day clinic in City in the North, waiting patiently for the doctor to remove the cast that was making my life a living hell. As he removed it, my foot just dropped down and I had no feeling in it at all. I fainted again. When I regained consciousness, the doctor said that I had lost 65% of the muscle power in my right leg and it would take some time to get used to it. I didn't initially understand what he meant by 'getting used to it.' The result of this operation was that I wasn't able to walk properly and had to go for a series of intensive physiotherapy sessions. It took six months for me to get more or less back to my old self and I never regained the muscle power that I had lost after the operation so I never went back for the operation on my other foot. After the operation, my right foot was a shoe size bigger than my left foot and I still struggle with that foot. The foot being too big results in my tripping and falling and because of this, most of my pants are torn at the knees and my hands are constantly bruised.

It was then that I realised that I would never be normal and would have to accept that my 'normal' was the way I was then and still am today. The way God had created me was *my* normal. If I try and make my body work the way other people think it should, I will trip and fall. I had to see and feel my own normal and realise that I don't have to be like everyone else in order to feel normal. As long as I don't have pain, feel happy and can do the things that I want to do, that is my normal. Let me give you an example; if you took my body and put it into a healthy body, into a body that has no muscular or nerve problems, I would be in pain. As I was born with the condition, I have never experienced what other people's 'normal' feels like. My normal is muscular dystrophy. If you took a normal, healthy body and put it into my body, that person would be in a tremendous amount of pain. The healthy body would have been used to experiencing 'normal feelings', changing it to a body with muscular dystrophy, would thus result in abnormal feelings.

By doing the operation on my foot, my own 'normal' that I'd grown accustomed to now became 'abnormal'. I currently limp badly on my right leg and people often ask me if I was in an accident or, 'Do you have a prosthesis?' I reply in the negative and explain that I have a muscular disease. Would I be walking better had the operation on my foot not been done? Did the operation result in me having more back and hip spasms?

The answer is 'Yes', it changed my normal to abnormal. I have accepted the way my body is now, I rewired my thinking into having a positive attitude towards the limp. I exercise regularly and have done rehabilitation exercises for the past 25 years. Exercise became a way of life for me. My advice to anyone would be the following: ***Give up the pain killers, don't operate if not necessary. Believe in exercise, it truly is medicine.***

As I approached the end of my school journey, I had grown as a person in many ways. In the last week of my school career I received a card from my class teacher. It read, 'Imagine you are a drop of water afloat in a loving sea; now ask yourself, where are my boundaries?' On reading this card again, I realised that I have never had many boundaries in my life.

When I did encounter boundaries, I always made a plan or found a solution to overcome them. ***It is important to identify your boundaries early and to never let them hold you back in life. Always strive to become extraordinary and push your boundaries to the limit. There is no boundary that can ever be too big, as long as you believe that anything is possible.***

Chapter Seven

Discovering Yourself

After my Grade 12 final exam, I packed my back pack and went to Europe for a year on a working holiday visa. Most youngsters I knew did that as a gap year, either to get working experience or to see the world while they are still young. My reasons were to get work experience, to become independent and to see the world before I became wheelchair bound. I did not then, and even now I still don't, imagine that I would still be able to walk, cycle or exercise.

My year in England helped me to develop into a very strong individual. I started off with a job as an au pair. But that did not last very long as I soon realised I could make more money being a full time waitron. Little did I know, however, that I would have to spend between 12 and 18 hours a day on my feet. As a result of 'walking funny' I don't have very good balance and the first cappuccino I had to carry to a table, fell onto the floor and broke into pieces. With the first bottle of wine I opened, I almost lost my finger when the corkscrew (waiter's friend) slipped and a cut my hand badly. The first plate of food I had to carry, burnt my arm. Not the most promising start to my life as a waitron!

I could not understand a word when I spoke to the first waiter I encountered because we were a very diverse bunch of people on the staff. There were Polish, Spanish, Turkish, Brazilian and even refugees from Yugoslavia as well as British people working on my team. It was not long before I realised that if you spoke Afrikaans, most people would understand at least part of what you said. I also encountered plenty of South Africans in England.

I was 18 years old and coming from a South African apartheid era background, I often felt as if I was in a movie. It didn't feel real. It was initially difficult for me to understand their 'normal' and I frequently had to say 'excuse me' or 'pardon me'. When I started understanding their reality, it became fun to work with a great bunch of people. We partied hard and worked even harder. We supported each other and shared our earnings. After about a month. I got better and better at my waitering skills. I became so good that at the end of that year, the company I worked for asked me to move into management. The General Manager who I worked for gave me his business card and I saw that the only things printed on it were the words General Manager, no name. I took the card and wrote my name in the blank space. I visualised myself in the position before I even had the title. Little did I know that six years later, I would indeed be a General Manager in a well-known fitness company. That business card stayed in my wallet for six years and every time I looked at it, the more driven I was to become it. I could see myself sitting in the General Managers office chair.

I waited on between six and nine tables at the same time. I made money and it helped that it was in pounds. To earn that money, though, I had to work my butt off. I had to put in long hours and spend all of them on my feet, which resulted in my developing sores on my feet. The bottom of my feet became rock hard as, after I finished a shift in the evenings, I had to walk another two kilometres home. Sometimes the only thing that worked for the pain in the middle of the night was a glass of Chardonnay. I would get home and soak my feet in warm water with soothing menthol vapours dissolved in it, just to cool them down. My lower back and legs would be in pain and I would think, 'Why am I doing this to myself?'

I was doing it because I wanted to succeed and to see what my body was capable of. I realised that my body could be as strong as my mind is. Every day I would wake up, put ointment on my legs and feet, listen to the song *'Who let the dogs out?'* get dressed and go to work. I was always on time and arrived before anyone else did, with my uniform neat and ironed.

At the end of that year, I travelled to six more countries. I visited my favourite cities in Europe, Budapest, Praha, Vienna, Amsterdam, London and Bratislava and I saw some of the world's finest landmarks. In London I saw Buckingham Palace, London Bridge, Westminster Abbey, Millennium Dome and Big Ben. I went punting on the Oxford University River and travelled to Brighton for a day with my best friend, Marco. He wanted me to see the Brighton Pier and the European ocean. I also travelled to Little Langdale in the Lake District to visit a school friend.

The highlight of my wild year was the Glastonbury festival. This is a big music festival that takes place on a farm in England in the middle of nowhere. We had one tent between eight people and had to sleep in shifts for two days. The tent was not used much as we carried on through the night, listening to amazing bands, artists and great jazz musicians. Even my favourite band, Counting Crows, was onstage at one time.

In Amsterdam I visited The Van Gogh Museum, the Rijksmuseum, the famous coffee shops and even the zoo. I admit that I did try out the weed as, what is a trip to Amsterdam without trying out their weed? I saw the amazing Keukenhof Gardens with their beautiful flowers. I love flowers and gardening and have green fingers so the Keukenhof experience was a breath-taking one for me. I even got a chance to see and experience the tulips of Amsterdam.

Marco and I decided that we wanted to travel Europe by car so we flew to Praha and rented a car for our trip. In Praha we went to the Praha Castle and the famous Charles Bridge. Marco convinced me to go the Praha Opera House to watch *Don Giovanni*. The opera was in Italian and I didn't understand a word of it but it was an interesting experience!

We didn't see much In Bratislava as the country had just come out of a war. The people looked poor and drained and it was quite a shocking experience to see what war can do to the psyche of a country. Slovakia and the Czech Republic were previously one country known as Czechoslovakia. After the war, they divided into two countries with different currencies.

Budapest consists of two parts, Buda and Pest. It is a beautiful city with friendly people, great beer and amazingly good food. At night the Night Bridge lights up the skies with beautiful lights. As you drift on a boat on the Danube River, you can see the amazingly constructed parliament house. The Citadella fortress watches out over Pest.

In a town named Karlovy Vary, we stayed over for a few nights in order to swim in the volcanic lagoon. At that time the Hungarian Grand Prix was on and we had the opportunity to participate in a competition to change the tyres on a real Ferrari Formula One racing car. It was awesome to do that! On the way from Budapest to Vienna, we got lost for six hours. A lady with a big shotgun almost shot us in a small village when we asked her for directions. When we crossed the border into Austria, we did not have the correct currency. We had no food or water and weren't able to buy anything without the correct money. We were extremely thirsty and hungry and a watermelon that we had bought at a market in Budapest saved our lives.

In Vienna we visited the St Peter's Cathedral and walked many kilometres in that city as we couldn't afford the public transport. We found Vienna to be a very expensive city. After two weeks of experiencing Europe by car, we went back to our English town of Berkhamsted.

When I realised that I only had three months left in Europe, I started saving money to send home to South Africa. I made enough money in those three months to buy a car and set myself up nicely as a student in South Africa.

I would like to share what I learnt from my experience of that year in Europe. I learnt to work with a diverse group of people from different countries and cultures and I made friends with people who were very different to me. I had to look after myself and make enough money to support what I wanted to achieve and do while I was away. I saw and experienced different food, beer and vibes in a variety of foreign cities. I took risks and challenged the norm. I grew up and I took responsibility for my life and my decisions.

What I would like to share with you is the following:

It is good to plan for your retirement but my advice is to not stop living your life today, to safeguard your future. Someday you might be old and have aches and pains and not be able to walk, hear, touch or even see anymore. When you are old and retired, you will probably not be able to see the world or do the things you always wanted to do. When you are old, you may only live to survive for the next day. All you need is a house, food and the means to pay your bills. Use your money now, do what you want to do now. Stop waiting for better days. Stop waiting for when you have enough money. Stop waiting for when the kids grow up. Do it now, get done what you want to do now. There might not be a tomorrow and the right time may never come.

Chapter Eight

Exercise is Medicine

I recall a day back in high school - it was just another day of doing very little when friends invited me to go and watch their field hockey game. Although I didn't understand the game that well, I was an avid supporter and knew when a goal had been scored! But knew nothing at all about game plans or the different roles and positions of players. As I was waiting on the side lines for the game to start, one of my friends came running up to me.

'We need a goalkeeper!' she said urgently. I looked at her and replied, 'Where should I go and look for her?'

'You won't find her anywhere. We don't have a goalkeeper, we want you to play.'

'You know I can't play any contact sports,' I responded. 'And I don't know what to do as a goalkeeper anyway. It would be better to have no one in the goals than to put me there.'

Next their coach approached me and said that all I needed to do was to put on the goalie kit and stand in the goal box. When the ball came my way, I should just kick it away.

'That sounds pretty easy,' I thought. I don't have to hit the ball, I can kick it. Nevertheless it took me 30 minutes to get dressed into the goalie kit. With padded shoes, huge shin pads, chest protector and helmet, I was dressed for action. If you looked at the body armour I had to put on, you would think I was preparing to be hit by a deadly ball. I was terrified and sweat was dripping from my forehead. I could feel my body going into shock from all the adrenalin pumping through my veins. I hadn't been this excited in a very long time. My only thoughts at that time were, 'You can do this. Stay alive, don't get killed.'

I was standing in the goal box trying to figure out what was going on when a girl came blasting through the middle of the field straight towards me. The first thing I thought of was 'Kick the ball.' But the girl had the ball on her stick so I ran forward and kicked the girl and the ball. She fell over and the ball went out. 'You saved it, Siekie!' came the cries from the team.

I did what? Saved what?

'They didn't score a goal! You saved it!' My team was screaming and laughing at the same time.

It felt good, it felt *really* good. My self-confidence was very high after that save. It was the first time I had touched the ball and I saved it from going into the goals! That is when I realised that it would be my job in the team to keep the ball out of the box. There were a few things I'd have to learn first, such as rules of the game and skills on how to be a goalkeeper was top on the priority list.

We won the game that day, my first game and we won! The other team did score a goal when the girl I had taken out the first time came back for her revenge. Winning felt very good and I knew that I really wanted more of this feeling. And guess what? I did not die, or break anything. I was still in one piece. The only pain that I had was the thought that they would not want me in their team. This was the under 14A team, surely they wouldn't put me in the A team after my first game of hockey?

After the game my team mates said that I had done really well, far better than they had expected me to. The coach asked me if I would like to play again and I answered with a big smile on my face, 'Yes, please.' I didn't look back after that day and began thinking about hockey constantly kept asking questions and started looking for someone who could teach me how to be a real goalie.

At the beginning of every year, our school held an athletics tournament. This happened just after our two weeks of initiation and I decided that I really did not want to sit around and do nothing on that day, as I had done the previous year when I'd been too scared to try anything.

My friends were very inspiring and encouraging and we decided that we would all participate in every event on that athletics day. The two weeks of initiation had made me realise that you have to try many things in life in order to find out what works for you and what fun it really can be. Although the activities were fairly hard core, as I described in Chapter Five, I did most of them and came out alive at the end of the day as a better person as I gained a sense of self-respect. We were still on a high and did everything as a team, as we had done during those two weeks of initiation. From Javelin throw to Shot Put to track events; each of us had an event that we were good at but we all tried everything. Some did high jump, I did low jump and fell on the cross bar while they jumped over it. With long jump, I landed before reaching the sand pit instead of landing in it, as you are supposed to. And the 100 meter dash, I came in dead last.

But in the Javelin throw I, surprised everyone, including myself, by coming first! In the Shot Put I came second and it felt amazing! Winning releases serotonin, the happy hormone, which makes you feel fantastic. If I had not tried everything, I would never have known that I'm actually good at some events. With my Javelin achievement, I made the athletics team and we travelled to the City in the North to compete against the schools there. We travelled everywhere and competed against some of South Africa's best schools. I met some great people on those trips who later became my best friends and I also had my first kiss on one of the trips. That first kiss was magic; it was at a dance we attended at the school we had competed against in a small town. I can't remember the name of the boy I kissed but I do remember that he had a big mouth that covered my entire face when he kissed me! After the kiss, we danced to a song called, *Bed of Roses* by *Bon Jovi* while my head was still up in the clouds.

What was more significant to me was meeting my goalie coach and mentor on that same athletics trip. I was becoming a person with real ambition and a strong desire to win and success started developing in me.

The Javelin coach was a guy with a real passion for the sport. He treated each of the athletes like a champion and always made me feel as if I was worthy. He made us train very hard at every single training session and it was all about perfecting the technique of throwing a javelin. The skill was in not pushing the javelin, but instead making it slide through the air. It was about finding your particular strength; the momentum you need to gain on the run-up, the speed with which you need to execute the perfect throw. If I relate what I did then to how I go about my role as a General Manager today, I know how well I paid attention then and I still treat every day as a Javelin training session. Just as I practised every day to perfect the technique of throwing a javelin, I need to perfect my technique and leadership skills in order to become a perfect leader. I need to make every single staff member feel like a champion. I need to show them the passion *I* have for my work. I need to show them that I love my work. I need to lead by example. *If you love what you do, you will never work a day in your life.*

The more I believed that I could achieve, the clearer it became to me that I really could do it. The more people told me that something was impossible, the more I wanted to show them that it was possible.

I started playing hockey for the under 14A girls team and we won the league in my first year of playing. The coach and mentor I had met on my athletics tour was coaching me once a week in her spare time. She was a real star on the hockey field and she became my role model and friend. She had passion both for the sport and for being a goalie and some of her passion rubbed off on me. The difference between us was that she had speed and balance while I had quick reflexes and a heart for being the best. She was an inspiring coach and assisted me greatly in developing my skills.

When she started coaching me she said that I had to stand on my toes the entire time as that makes your reaction time in stepping forward and kicking the ball much quicker. Because I do not have good balance, I wasn't able to stand on my toes so I had to improvise and would stand more or less on my toes with my knees bent. I definitely did not have quick feet but what I did have was great perseverance, vision and very fast reflexes. She taught me how to use what I had to make me the best at what I was doing. She coached and mentored me so well that year that I very quickly learnt the techniques and rules of the game. When I was 15 years-old I was selected to play with my mentor and coach for the school's first hockey team, quite an achievement for someone who had only played for a year! Another important skill I learnt from her was how to coach and mentor people to become as good as, or even better than, you are. Leaders mentor and coach other leaders; if you don't develop people you are not leading, you are following. She knew that she was finishing her school career that year and that the school needed a new goalie. She played most of the games for the first team but I got the opportunity to practise with her and to see what see did. That gave me that self-confidence that I needed to take over the position from her.

I learnt something new in every practise session and I gradually became fitter and stronger. I could see myself going far in the sport and, despite the disadvantages of my condition, I became better than I had been at the sport. When I was on the field playing hockey, I felt normal, I felt as if I was just like the other players. I might not have had the speed and balance they had, but I did have the guts and this made me as competitive and strong as they were.

I am proud to be able to say that I stood in a goal box and faced balls from the best 'striker' and top goal scorer in women's hockey in the world, even though I only saved two of the 50 shots she sent flying my way. When one of the balls she hit struck my goalie boot, it felt like needles and pins in my feet, as if I had been shot in the toe. Although it was sore, I was just proud of having saved a ball that she had hit. Who would have thought then that she would still be playing for South Africa today and that she would be the best striker and top goal scorer in the world and would hold a Guinness world record for the most goals scored in a career? She is the legend of field hockey.

Looking back at what I learnt from her and what I still see today in her character, I can confidently say that she is humble, loves the game and is fully committed and proud to be a South African. I learnt from the best to become the best. I knew in my hockey years that I wouldn't be able to become a Springbok hockey player, but I promised myself that I would not be average. I wanted to be extraordinary. I wanted to play with the big guns. I surrounded myself with great athletes in order to feel like a great athlete.

I never stopped exercising and when I started working in the health and wellness industry, it was not about the job. It was about the lifestyle and about exercise being medicine.

My dad bought me a bicycle when I turned 15 as he realised that I needed more exercise and I was getting really busy with all my outdoor activities. When the school bell rang for the end of the school day, I had to run to the hostel to get dressed in my afternoon sports gear. I would then run to the dining room, grab some food and head out the door for the afternoon's activities. . I had 15 minutes to cycle eight kilometres, with my big goalie kitbag on my back, to the university where I was doing my rehabilitation exercises. The bag was as big as I was and weighed about 10kg but I became a master at cycling with it and grew really strong minded. Uphill was crunch time and I'd tell myself, 'Don't look at how far you still have to go, focus on where you are.' Pedal by pedal I slowly moved up the hill with my massive bag on my back. Downhill you could feel the blood is surging through your veins, your breath came fast and your heart rate was very high. 'Focus on your breathing. Try to take deep breaths to slow your breathing down a little.'

When my parents and gran heard that I was cycling 15 kilometres a day with a 10kg bag on my back, they felt sorry for me. On my sixteenth birthday I had a surprise waiting for me in my room on the farm; they had bought me a 60cc motorcycle. I was ecstatic and from there on it was only downhill. It was a big decision for my parents to trust me with a motorcycle. They said they never doubted me being responsible, but they doubted irresponsible motorists on the road.

Always remember those who had an impact on your life

I was delighted to receive my Provincial colours for hockey at the age of 16. We travelled far that year for IPT's (national championships). We came third in that tournament, but yet I received the prize for having the most team spirit and for creating fun. The year I was 17, we also travelled to a town in the middle of nowhere to play the national tournament on grass turf which wasn't that nice as I was used to playing on Astroturf. In my last year of school and hockey, we travelled to the northern parts of the country and I will never forget that trip, not for the tournament but for the tragedy that occurred.

As we arrived in town, we received the news that the under 16A team had been in a terrible road accident on their way to their IPT; the front wheel of their bus had burst and sent them rolling off the road. Many of my best friends were on that bus. It was a tragic accident and most of the girls sustained serious injuries. The head girl of one of the schools passed away on the scene of the accident.

After a week in the trauma unit, my best friend died, due to the result of severe head trauma. According to the girls who were in the crash, she fell out of the bus about 50 meters from where it ended up. She had still been walking around on the scene trying to help the others but after a while she just went and sat down. That was when she went into a coma that she never woke up from.

She was a fantastic friend and a great hockey player, always friendly and with a big smile on her face. I can still remember the sound of her laugh, a loud and sincere laugh. She always said, 'If we put our problems in God's hands, there is nothing we need to understand. It is enough to just believe, that what we need, we will receive.'

She was a great example of a humble and generous human being. 'If we live truly, we shall truly live' was the quote on her burial service hand out. She will always be in my heart and thoughts. I will never forget her and I'm still sad that she was taken from us at such a young age. Thank you for being a part of my life even if it was only for a short while. What I learnt from you and the support you gave me as a friend will be with me for the rest of my life. Riding my bicycle 10 kilometres to visit you, was never too far. The values of friendship that you taught me will guide me to make the right choices with friends every day.

So what did I learn from that experience? I think the main lesson from that tragedy was, *'If we think about how unpredictable life is, we should really be writing our obituaries today in order to see if we are truly living or merely existing.*

How will people remember you? What legacy would you like to leave? How many people will attend your funeral? These are all questions you should be asking yourself daily to measure your worth and make sure you live for each and every moment.

How long will people remember you after your last day on earth? Will any of your friends write about you in their books 18 years after your death?

Challenge yourself – Lift your Lid continually

Mountain biking became a hobby of mine at the age of 32. The regional General Managers of my area decided to enter the most Challenging mountain bike race ever. We cycled the very challenging race together and had so much fun. Although I walked most of the race, I finished it but there were times during that race when I wanted to give up, when I just wanted to turn around and quit. Halfway up the mountain, I could really feel my life flashing before my eyes as it was extremely hot and the terrain was way above my skill level. As I got to the top of the mountain, I saw an ambulance and all I wanted to do was to throw my bike down and go and sit in it. I asked myself why I had decided to torture my body so much, what did I want to prove by this cycling? As I looked back, I saw the massive mountain that we had just conquered. 'We did this!' I thought to myself. 'Two months ago I would not have had the strength and/or energy to do this but today I did it.' I had trained hard for the race and I realised that if I quit at that point, I would have to ride all the way back to the start. 'I may as well continue,' I mentally told myself. 'I want to finish this race; it can only be downhill from here on.'

As I sailed down the mountain, adrenaline was pumping and I was so excited. I was going down at 38 km/h. Focused on the road ahead of me I felt the wind rushing past me. I felt good, really good! My heart was pumping. In the distance I could see a water point, 'Finally,' I thought to myself 'I need ice water and sugar.' As I got to the water point, the guy there said, 'Don't worry, it's only downhill from here on, only 10 kilometres to go.' It felt as if I had already done 60 kilometres but when I looked at my speedometer, I realised that I had only finished nine kilometres of the race. I was devastated. As I continued the race, my legs were burning and my heart was working hard. As I came around a bend, I saw another mountain. 'Am I on the right track?' I wondered. The person at the water point had just said that it was downhill from there but this was definitely not downhill. I wanted to start crying. I got off my bike and started pushing it again. I could feel the pain in my back getting worse and the intense heat was just sapping every last bit of energy from me. 'You will *not* give up Siekie! You are not a quitter. You are better than this. You will finish. You can do this. You have enough energy!' Those words were going through my mind. As I was saying this to myself, I could feel how slowly I started to walk and how heavy my body became. Just when I felt I wanted to faint, I heard this small voice next to me. It was a 12 year-old boy.

'Are you okay? Can I push your bike for you?' he asked. I looked at this boy and thought to myself, 'If he can do this race at such a young age, I can do it!' As I looked around me I could see many people struggling. Everyone was having difficulty completing the race; fat and thin, fit and unfit. I took a sip of water and continued up the mountain. The terrain became more technical as we got closer to the end and my body was close to shutting down. When I saw the finish line, I was not just happy, I was relieved. I had made it. It was only 20km but to me it had felt like at least 60km!

My friends were crossing the finish line one after the other and all of them looked and felt the same way I did. Their faces were red and they were exhausted. It was great to see how each of them had also pushed themselves above their limits. The one friend has chronic asthma and I could hear her chest was whistling as she really struggled to get air. It was amazing to see her crossing the finish line. Another colleague, was such a team player and had waited for and assisted the struggling bunch through the entire race. She motivated them to push forward and to finish the race. For the one lady, this was also a special race as it was only her second time on a mountain bike. After cycling five kilometres, she was excited to discover that the bike had gears! Inexperienced and completely taken out of her comfort zone, she completed the race. Aimee finished the race ahead of us, although the fact that she is bipolar makes life a constant challenge. Her thoughts are in constant battle and argument with her body and her mind is always telling her that she is a failure and worthless. She did not listen to any voices that day; she remained strong and completed the race.

I completed three mountain bike races in three weeks in 2014. It was an accomplishment that I could really acknowledge myself for. I was proud of myself and showed myself what my body is capable of doing and also showed my colleagues, friends and family what can be done. Most importantly, I showed myself that I am normal in my own way, that I can achieve anything as long as I believe and have perseverance. There have been many instances in my life where I conquered challenging mind and body events. The reason why this was such an accomplishment for me was that I was then 32 years old. Most cynics had told me that I would be in a wheelchair by the age of 18 due to muscle degeneration and that I would be lucky if I got to celebrate my 30th birthday. I guess that I can consider myself lucky. I have realised that I have my entire life in front of me and I create my own luck by believing in myself, my capabilities and my spirit. There is still so much living to do for me. It feels as if my life has just started.

Exercise is not just medicine, it is a means of preventing illnesses. With the correct exercise, you can decrease your pain. Instead of taking pain medication, first try to do exercise. If health professionals could start prescribing exercise instead of pills or medication, I believe that the world would change for the better. There is no quick fix to being healthy. There is no quick diet. There is no pill that can make you lose weight fast without you doing the work by exercising. Everything takes time, invest in your health.

You need to do the work, you need to get up and get active.

Chapter Nine

Be Yourself, Everyone Else is Taken

The way you see the world is a reflection of the way you have been taught to see it. From the time you were a small child, you were trained and conditioned to believe certain things. For example, you were probably told to fit into the crowd and behave like everyone else. You were told not to sing too loudly when you are happy and not to dream too big when you are feeling inspired. You learnt that those who are different wouldn't be accepted and that conformity would lead to success. You were taught not to speak your truth and to not be too loving, otherwise you would be taken advantage of. You were taught that possessions and external power would bring you lasting happiness.

I bought into the world's belief system. I wanted to be the perfect child to my parents. I wanted to be the perfect sister to my brother. I wanted to be the perfect grandchild to my Granny.

I wanted to become what the world wanted me to be, what society says is right and what the media shows the world. Yet the normal of what the world was trying to teach me and my own normal differed completely. I was scared that the world would reject me for not doing and believing what it expected of me to. I was scared that I would get to the end of my life not living my own life, but living the life my parents, society or teachers wanted me to. I was scared that when I got to the last hour of my last day, I would realise that I had lived society's life because I didn't have the guts, the courage to live my own life.

I made a choice to surround myself with books about people who changed the world. I started studying why Nelson Mandela had been such a great leader. Before he went to prison, Mandela was an angry man. He came out of prison 27 years later a changed man because of his inner work, his studying and his reflection on life; he came out as the Nelson Mandela South Africa got to know. He taught me that my outer life mirrors my inner life. The day Mandela died, the world came to South Africa to mourn. Many kings, queens, presidents, princes and princesses, businessmen and women, even millionaires and movie stars paid tribute to the legacy that he left. He was the father of our nation and changed the way South Africans think. He brought equality to a country that was unfair and racist. Despite all the change that has happened, I realise that it is going to take longer than anybody anticipated for the mind-set and values of South Africans to change. We all say we are equal, but are we really living that belief out? Are we really talking it? Are we really not racists?

I started surrounding myself with positive people. I had to rewire my thinking. I had to start thinking differently.

George Bernard Shaw wrote: 'The reasonable man adapts himself to the world, the unreasonable one persists in adapting the world to himself. Therefore all progress depends on the unreasonable man.'

The world caused me to adapt myself, my dreams, my values and who I really am to it. The world put blinkers over my eyes. I learnt that if I was honest with myself, I would need to start being unreasonable. I would need to reverse-hypnotise myself and would have to change the way the world taught and shaped me. I had to start thinking towards being the person that I wanted to be and who I wanted to become. I could no longer live with telling my parents and brother lies. It was very difficult for me to speak to them and not be able to tell them stories about the person whom I loved. It was difficult because the world shaped and formed my parents and brother the way society and the world wanted each human to be. My father was a farmer and my mother a housewife. Their perception about the world and what I wanted to tell them was going to rip their worlds apart. I thought about doing this many times and judged myself many times as being selfish.

How can I be so selfish and hurt my parents and brother like that? I was looking for answers in the Bible. I read books and tried to find ways in which to make the entire process a win-win situation for both my parents and myself. No matter what I did to try and change myself into being 'straight,' nothing worked. Not kissing men and doing extreme things with them to prove to myself that I was 'straight, not going out to clubs, bars and places where there were different men to choose from. I would kiss them, play with them and sometimes take them home with me. But nothing worked.

Every time I woke up in my own bed the next morning, I felt empty and disappointed in myself. I was disappointed for drinking too much and for kissing a complete stranger. At one New Year's party, I kissed 16 men in one night. I can remember how many men I kissed, but I cannot for the life of me remember any of their names. If I had enjoyed the kissing, I would most probably not have kissed 16 men in one night. For 18 years of my life, I really tried to be 'straight.' I tried to be the person the world wanted me to be. Someone said not so long ago, that the only reason I became gay was because of the fact that I have muscular dystrophy. She said that the way I walk would make it difficult for me to find a man and that it would be hard to find a man who didn't want children. As I said earlier in the book, I would not want to bring a child into the world knowing that he or she would struggle with an illness which is really hard to live with.

I know that this is not the reason why I am gay. I simply came to understand that there is no point in explaining something so intricate to someone if they are only willing to understand it from their own perspective. Their thinking is their own reality and it is what makes them happy.

There is no reason or life experience that makes you gay. You are born gay. You have this longing for something that is not normal with regard to what you've been brought up to believe and be. There is this constant feeling that you have to fight against when a woman is really attractive and gives you a butterfly feeling in your stomach. When your best friend makes you really happy and you want to act on how she makes you feel. When you fight the feelings for years and then realise one day that the feelings are actually mutual. It is when you get so jealous when your best friend goes out with guys and makes out with them. It is when you tell your best friend that no guy will ever be right for her. It is when you watch all of this, drinking yourself into oblivion to accept that the world wants you to kiss guys and make out with strangers in order for you to fit into it. And then you get to the point in your life, where you can't take it to see your best friend kiss other people, any longer. It is when you make the decision to act on that burning feeling to kiss a woman. Trust me when I tell you that after I kissed a woman for the first time, I never looked back.

Being labelled as gay can either make or break you. As human beings, we all label people in different ways but at the same time we also long to fit in and belong. Normal humans call themselves straight and think they do everything correctly. They think that they are perfect. The only reason why we label people is for us to fit into our own normal.

I was shocked when I realised that humans are mean and I'll share this story with you. A white man came to me one day and talked about an accident that had happened on the N1 highway. I was standing next to another white male as the guy told us about the car crash and that 18 people had died. The man standing next to me then asked the following question, 'Were they blacks?' The guy telling the story replied, 'Yes most of them were black.' The other guy responded, 'Blacks don't know how to drive, that is why they get killed.' I was shocked to hear that people can think like that. Why would humans label black people as bad drivers? Why would humans label black people as thieves? Why would humans label black people for being illiterate? Is it the colour of your skin that makes people label you? Is it because you don't look like they do, think or drive the way they do? Do you deserve to die because of that? It made me realise that the human race will never change, they want everyone to think and be the same. They want everybody to fit into their world. Maybe it is time for *them* to adjust and adapt to change. I think it is time that we find a balance in the world. I think it is time that we stop judging people and instead start loving more. Stop hating, start inspiring.

A few years ago HIV became known as the 'silent killer'. Some people labelled HIV as an illness that only black people could get. The older black people said that only the younger generation could get HIV. The reality is that HIV is an illness that anyone can contract at any age or stage of their lives. It doesn't matter if you are black or white or if you are young or old. For many years, HIV was labelled as an illness that only gay men could get so that when people saw a gay guy, they would assume that he had HIV/Aids. It has been very hard for me to accept this but the fact is that humans are mean.

God wants us to love him unconditionally. How can we love God unconditionally if we cannot love, respect and accept each other unconditionally? It does not matter how much the world changes, God remains constant. He doesn't love us less because we are black or white, he doesn't stop loving us because we are gay, He doesn't stop loving someone because they have HIV, and He doesn't stop loving a person because they are an alcoholic. God loves every single person on this earth. Let's start loving each other and helping each other to survive in this cruel world. Let's change this cruel world into a place of love and happiness.

I'll come back now to how I made the decision to tell my parents that I am gay and to accept the consequences of this and to live with the choice I have made for the rest of my life. My mom was very supportive and understanding and said that God loves me for who I am. She also told me that she will love me unconditionally for who I am, whatever my choice is. Although it was very hard for her, she understood. I knew that she had wanted me to have a white wedding and to have children. But she said that she had always known deep inside her that it was never going to happen. She knew that I was different, not only because I have muscular dystrophy but she always felt that my best friends and I were just a little *too c*lose.

Baby boomers grew up in an era where being gay was not tolerated and apartheid was the norm in South Africa. The majority of Baby boomers will never accept gay people or the new political ways. What they will do is to live with the situation. We cannot judge them for the way they think, that is their reality. They were conditioned by the world's beliefs when they grew up. When the world changed, they were forced to change with the world. Baby boomers were not left with much of a choice; all the change was a big shock to them.

The night I told my dad I am gay, we both had a lot to drink. The big farmer started crying and I was crying as if someone had died. The next morning, I not only had a huge hangover but also had a headache of gigantic proportions. My eyes felt as if they wanted to fall out of my head. My mom came to lie with me on my bed and brought me cucumber to put on my eyes. It works like a bomb to put cold cucumber on your eyes when you have cried a lot. She held me tightly in her arms and whispered, 'I love you and everything will be fine.' I was relieved to hear her say that.

My dad did not say much. He rejected what I had told him and said that it was not true. He said I would get over it. It's been many years since I told my parents and I'm still not over it.

I have great friends, highly motivated and driven people. We will do anything for each other and we are very supportive. On our birthdays we have great get togethers, where we make lovely food and talk for hours. We laugh a lot and talk about things that made a difference in our lives. We all have nicknames, most of them given by me. I only give nicknames to people I like so if they don't have a nickname, there is something seriously wrong.

Our group of friends has come a long way and has been through tough times in our personal lives. We know that the group will always stand together and help each other when needed. If you listen to everyone's life story, you will understand why I say this. We are a group of gay women living our lives to the fullest and are open minded individuals who listen to each other and to the perspectives of other people. We care and we give back to our communities.

A couple got married in February 2013 and it was the most beautiful wedding. The one lady's dad is a Dutch Reformed Church minister and he conducted the ceremony. They were not allowed to get married in her dad's church as it was against their rules for gays to get married in the Dutch Reformed Church.

I'm going to share what he spoke about on their wedding day. He started by praying to the Lord and said that it was a privilege to have everyone present to share the wonderful day in God's presence. We are all children of God and are safe in His hands. He thanked God for his word and that it is open to everybody. He thanked God for keeping his word simple so that we can all understand it and that it is not made up of unrealistic laws.

He preached about being gay and about gay marriage. When his daughter first told him that she is gay, he and his wife thought that it was going to be easy. They didn't think that it was going to be difficult until their daughter told them that she wanted to get married. Her father thought that this was never going to happen but it had a big influence on their lives and they started thinking about her plans. He said that there are some things in life that you don't think about but, as soon as something has an impact on your life, you start thinking about it.

'This is not a gay wedding,' he said, 'it is two people who fell in love with each other.' He did not expect anyone to understand or accept this concept immediately as he had struggled with it for a long time himself. He had found an answer for himself and did not want to use the Bible to make him feel good about his decision. He did not want to be the person known for changing the Bible to suit himself and would not do that. He wanted to search for an honest answer and emphasised that he did not want to change the word of God. He wanted the Bible to give him a believable answer that also makes spiritual sense, something that is logical and understandable to everyone. The key to this matter is MORAL principles, he said. Everything can change as long as the principles don't change and every law has principles. Principles are the reason for the laws and without principles the laws mean absolutely nothing.

When the apostles asked what the most important commandment is, Jesus replied that it is not about the most important commandment, it is rather about love for God.[2] That you need to love God is the main principle around the commandment; you need to love God with your whole heart, soul and all your knowledge. Without love you are nothing. God is the beginning of everything and we need to start with Him. God stays God and even if everything in life changes, He remains God. The Lord is an Almighty God filled with love and care. He forgives people for their sins because Jesus died to pay for our sins. God loved the world so much that he gave his only Son to die for our sins. Everything in the Bible is God's word. We must not delete certain things because we feel like it. We must take everything in the Bible and live our lives according to it.[2]

The Bible has many verses containing facts but there are some verses in the Bible that are not factual. Sometimes they contain stories or parables that are open to interpretation. The stories are about having a relationship with God and about trusting Him. Everything in the Bible is the truth. God gave his son Jesus to the world, not to judge the world but for the world to be saved by Jesus.

He used the example of when people had to wear hats to church. According to the Bible, you had to wear a hat to show respect in church. If you did not wear a hat, you would be considered to be disrespectful and were looking for trouble. Nowadays you no longer have to wear a hat to show respect. The world changes but God stays constant. Long ago when a woman walked into a meeting without covering her head, she would be considered disrespectful and would be pressing the wrong buttons of the people in the meeting. The principles remain and it is about trust and respect for one another. Whether you do or don't wear a hat, the principle of trust and respect stay the same. You can leave the hat off; it is not about the hat. It is about the principle.

In the times when Paul was preaching, they said that women were not allowed to preach the word of God. That woman are not intelligent enough, they compared women's intelligence to that of a child. Would we still say that today?

---

[2] English Standard Version
John 13:34 -'A new commandment I give to you, that you love one another: just as I have loved you, you also are to love one another'.

Working on Sundays was another example he used in his sermon. Jesus said that Sunday is a day of rest, it is there for people to choose to rest and to find balance in their lives. Some people choose to work on a Sunday and today most businesses are open on Sundays. Again the world changes but God stays the same.

When it comes to marriage, God states that it is not good that humans are alone. God's solution to this is that he will make someone for each person and that person will be able to help and fit together thus God will give each person a soul mate. The principle is to have someone who loves you. Not just for straight people, but also for gay people. It is not good for humans to be alone.

In 2015, the Dutch Reformed Church changed the church law regarding gay marriage and now allows gay couples to get married. The church has come a long way since I came out as gay. Did the church do this to allow all individuals to be equal? Or did the church change the law to try and change the gay people's ways into becoming straight?

My two beautiful friends gave birth to a beautiful little girl a year after they got married. She will be growing up in a very diverse world and with the guidance of these two wonderful ladies who have high moral values, she will become an extraordinary individual. This little girl was christened in the Dutch Reformed Church by her grandfather, the same grandfather who had not been allowed to perform his own daughter's marriage ceremony in his church. I cried on the day of the christening, a wonderful ceremony. All the people attending were happy and joyful. Instead of breaking people down, the church is starting to inspire people and build them up. The road to equality is one step closer.

To make everything just so much more exciting, my friends had a boy!

Falling in love

I met my Aimee at the Gym and I'm going to say it again…My life, my career, my passion and everything that makes me happy, began at the Gym.
When I arrived at work one morning in 2007, I saw this new casual in reception. She looked very shy and uncertain. I greeted her and immediately thought; 'She's gay.'

I didn't initially give her much attention. There was a girl visiting her in reception daily during her shifts and I didn't want to interfere in their relationship. This was six months after my break-up with my previous girlfriend whom I had dated for three years. I was devastated when that relationship ended but little did I know that it was the best thing that could have happened to me. It took me a while to get over the break-up and I did some heavy drinking and smoking, but not much eating at that time. Even during the relationship I didn't have many aspirations or goals that I wanted to achieve. I was a binge drinker and used to go to work without having a purpose. I got stuck in administration as an admin manager for four years before I was promoted to Operations Manager. I was in a relationship that was not at all good for me. I will never take away from the fun we had in the three years we were together and if I say that I can't remember much of the love, it is because I was drunk most of the time. I was irresponsible and did a lot of clubbing, drinking and driving.

In the six months that I was single, I got even worse. There was no one to go home to. My ex never slept over during the week but she visited me every night for three years and on weekends she slept over. I hated it every single time she had to go home in the evening, even though we fought a lot. I had reason to have trust issues and in our three years together, it was very difficult for me to trust her. She disappointed me a few times and I don't think I'm ready to write about that yet.

As I had to walk past Aimee every day I couldn't stop thinking about her. As I was filing and getting her personnel file ready, I did some investigating into who she was. As I read the file, I saw that she was busy doing her Master's degree in Microbiology. I was immediately drawn to this girl more than ever before. She wasn't only beautiful, shy and had a lovely smile, but she was also intelligent and had a great deal of knowledge. I picked up my phone and sent her a poem via text messaging. The poem was about a butterfly, she still remembers the poem today. She did not have my number at that stage but I had her number because I was the admin manager. I ended the poem off with a number six as my friends called me Six or Siekie. It took her about six hours to find out who '6' was. She then messaged me back, 'Do you want to go for drinks at *the bar* tonight?' I said yes, of course!

I had an appointment with my parents that night so I ended up being late for my date. Three hours late. Trust me when I tell you that she still remembers that I made her wait for three hours on our first date. As I walked into *the bar* I saw her standing at the bar. I picked her up when I hugged her and we immediately went to sit at a table and started talking. It was not long before I kissed her in a 'straight' bar. I don't do that. People were apparently staring at us but I couldn't have cared less. I couldn't stop looking into her eyes and when she was quiet, I would kiss her. We eventually left the bar and went to my car. She is still too shy to talk about what happened in the car that night. We didn't look back after that. She moved into my townhouse a month after that night.

After our night of romance, it was very hard for me to concentrate at work the next day. Aimee (not her real name) walked into my office at 10 the next morning with a squash racket in her hand. I looked at her and said: 'Really? You want to play squash after last night' She went blood red 'No' she said 'I had to find a reason to come to see you without looking like a stalker.' I stood up, went to my manager and said that I had stomach cramps and wanted to go home. She gave me permission to leave.

Aimee and I spent the entire day chatting and so on…She only told me a year later that she had been very frightened about the gay thing and that I was her first real relationship. The other girl had been more of a drinking partner and not much more. Or so she said.

We were together for a week before she told me that she had booked a holiday months previously to go to the coast with her friend and was planning to go for two weeks. I was so in love at that stage that I couldn't see myself without her for even a day. As she got onto the bus to go on her holiday, I started crying as if I was saying farewell for a year. We chatted daily for hours on 'Mixit,' and phoned each other up to three times a day. One night she asked how I felt about our relationship. I replied, 'I love you. I think I can love you for the rest of my life.' The very next day she was on the bus back to The city although she'd only had about five days of her two week holiday. I was eagerly waiting at the bus station three hours before the bus arrived. I thought that if I sat and waited, the time would go faster.

When she got into the car I felt this warm feeling in my stomach. I felt happy, alive and ready to take on this journey of love. She looked at me and smiled. She had such a sincere and lovely look on her face that made me want to kiss her for as long as I could. I didn't give her much time to speak, all I heard was 'Hello'. After that I was busy kissing the woman I loved for as long as I could. She eventually said, 'It is almost morning, don't you think it is time to go home?'

We were joined together with love and passion and had our bad and good times. Most of the time was adventurous and fun and we never stopped looking for ways to have an adventure together. We always looked for things that could push our boundaries. And we did it so well together.

She accepted me for who I am and muscular dystrophy became part of our lives. What we didn't know was that she also had something holding her back in life. When I met her I realised that she was on anti-depressants. It was weird for me to see someone with a normal body and everything functioning normally to be on anti-depressants. I thought that they were only for people with a physical disabilities or who had lost a limb in an accident.

I told her to stop taking her tablets as I thought that would help her cope with life's challenges and show her that pills are not the way to go. We never missed a party and drank and smoked a lot. Most of the time when we drove home, we were drunk; we can thank our guardian angels that we are alive today. I want to write about one specific period here. It was about four years into our relationship when I realised, she could not function effectively without anti-depressants. She started having blackouts while she was driving and her mood swings damaged our relationship badly. She became very jealous and selfish. She also explained to me that it was very hard for her to wake-up in the mornings to go to work. I started noticing that she was sleeping a lot and that she rarely spoke to me anymore. She had this dead look in her eyes.

71

If I didn't cook, there would be no meal. She started shopping as if she had all the money in the world. She created debts for herself and when she reached the point where she realised that there was no way out and that she couldn't afford things anymore, everything just became too much for her.

One day she told me that had she made an appointment with a psychologist and was going to book herself into a mental institution. At first it was very hard for me to grasp the concept of a chemical imbalance in her head and I couldn't understand why she was making her life so complicated. She was normal, beautiful and had a Master's degree in Microbiology. 'How can she be depressed?' I thought?

She was diagnosed with bipolar disorder. I had no idea what the disease was or what to expect but I learnt that bipolar disorder is a mental disorder characterized by extreme shifts in mood, as well as fluctuations in energy and activity levels. During these abnormal shifts, the patient commonly finds it difficult to complete everyday tasks. Bipolar disorder is also known as manic-depressive illness.

It is a serious mental illness that can destroy relationships, undermine career prospects, and seriously affect academic performance. The American Psychological Association says that these emotional shifts can become so overwhelming that individuals may choose suicide.

The hardest part for me was to see how she went through the different episodes. One minute she would be feeling on top of the world, exhilarated or euphoric and the next minute she would have a feeling of gloom, blackness, despair, and hopelessness. She would go into extreme sadness, where it was mostly impossible to get her out of that state. The only thing that made her happy was sweets and chocolates; she became an emotional eater.

Her thoughts came and went rapidly (racing thoughts) and sometimes bizarre ideas came to her mind, and were acted upon. This might involve, for example, attempting to redo the plumbing in the house or rearranging everything in the fridge in order to solve a totally unrelated matter. She would start projects, from woodworking, beading, exercise and diets, and never finish them. Every time she started a new hobby, she would spend money on it; she would squander money on things that were of no benefit to us or our home.

During the manic episodes she had concentration difficulties and became easily distracted. She would find it very hard to complete her work and struggled to focus on her work and even going in to work was difficult for her. It took constant motivation from me to remind her how great she is.

Insomnia and sleeping problems - difficulty falling asleep, or falling asleep and waking up during the night and then not being able to get back to sleep, or sleeping much more than usual - were also an issue. During this phase she spent most of her time in bed. She would cry in her sleep at night and when I woke her up to comfort her, she would say that the 'Grim Reaper' had come to collect her. She had very bad nightmares almost every night. I couldn't imagine how bad that must have been.

Every second week we had to go on a new diet. We would lose weight but a month later; we would gain it all back again. She would start exercising rapidly and intensely for about three weeks and would then fall back into a state of not wanting to do anything.

She got irritated easily; this could be triggered by noises, smells, tight clothing, and other things that she could usually tolerate or ignore. If a place was too busy, she would not go into it.

Living with someone with bipolar is a challenge. Living with anyone who suffers from depression is also a challenge. The person with the disease does not realize how hard it is to live with and understand the way they are thinking and feeling. Yes, we all know it is caused by a chemical imbalance but as life partners we want to help, assist and try to make the sufferer feel better. In the process of trying to fix things, we often make them worse. We say things like, 'Get over the mood, what are you depressed about, get yourself back on track.' This just drives the depressed person to be more depressed. We do not mean to do it, but we act the way we do due to three things:

If we cannot pay money to get something fixed, we feel powerless. If we cannot fix things with our hands, we feel incompetent. If we cannot speak and tell people how to think because that works for us, we become impatient.

By doing this we drive people away from us. We want to be in control, but we are not.

We have to accept that we cannot change people who are depressed. We have to let them be their own person and accept that if they take their medication, they will be fine. There are professional doctors who can help them. Don't try to be their doctor. Just be their partner. Just allow them to live.

Aimee was different when she came out of the mental institution. She said that she was now prepared to make drastic changes to her lifestyle and relationships. The first thing she stopped doing was smoking. I followed her example and also stopped smoking. Then she stopped drinking strong liquor and still only drinks a glass or two of wine or a beer. She started taking medication for her disorder and she got better.

Even with all the challenges related to her bipolar disorder, she is the most loving, kind, friendly and interesting person that I know. She has a very high skill-set in almost everything and she loves taking on new projects. Most of the time I had to push her to finish projects but we knew each other so well and she has great values. I loved Aimee not for who she is, I loved her for how she made me feel when I was with her.

This is how I will always remember Aimee, through the following poem she wrote me:

I do not love you as if you were salt-rose, or topaz,

Or the arrow of carnations the fire shoots off.

I love you as certain dark things are to be loved, in secret, between the shadow and the soul.

I love you as the plant that never blooms but carries in itself the light of hidden flower; thanks to your love a certain solid fragrance, risen from the earth, lives darkly in my body.

I love you without knowing how, or when, or from where. I love you straight forwardly, without complexities or pride; so I love you because I know no other way.

Than this: where I do not exist, nor you, so close that your hand on my chest is my hand, so close that your eyes close as I fall asleep.

And this I vow to you – my love is yours forever. My every decision, my every move will be made, keeping you and us in my mind, so that pain and hurt will be prevented and happiness on both sides are kept and we will be happy.

You are my heart, my soul and I love you always.

'Play to your partner's strengths. Do not focus too much on their weaknesses.' It is important to focus on what you want to achieve as a couple through each other's strengths. There are so many beautiful characteristics in each human being. If you can see the good in your partner, you will not focus on their weaknesses.

Chapter Ten

Happiness

My friends moved to a farm just outside the city in 2010. It wasn't easy at first but with the support of their group of friends, the farm is now a lovely place. When they moved into the house there was no electricity or running water there. It was very dusty and there were lots of bushes outside. We would spend nights in the empty farm house. With there being no toilet, we had to do our business in the veldt. This was always a big laugh as one by one we would take turns to sit on a wheelbarrow's edge. When you were finished doing your number one, you had to move the wheelbarrow forward so that the next person could use it. Some nights it was very cold to sit outside on a wheelbarrow and there was a horse that was also lurking around the house at night. While you would sit doing your thing, you would hear the neigh of this massive horse right next to you. If you were caught with your pants around your ankles, you would eat dust; face first into the ground. Don't try and run away from the horse.

We would look at the stars through a telescope and we would talk about things that we did not know much about. One night my friend and I had a little too much whisky and we spent about two hours looking at the stars, discussing what we saw. Another friend then joined us and pointed out that the lens of the telescope was still closed. 'How the hell have you spent two hours looking at the stars while the lens was still closed?' she asked. We burst out laughing and couldn't stop laughing for a long time. It wasn't about looking at the stars, it was about talking about things in life that mattered, something other than work and problems.

We had many good times on the farm and even helped to plant the grass. Not the best work we've ever done, but at least we tried. The grass was still uneven after three years. The day we planted the grass was hot as hell and I had sunburn and blisters on my hands at the end. We had so much fun that day; everyone worked hard to get the grass planting finished before the end of the day. We did finish planting the grass and that piece of grass has character. Whenever my friends look at the grass, they see the hard work of their friends and also the love that went into getting everything green on the farm. They worked really hard to get their farm to where it is today. For two women it can be a real challenge to run a small farm yet they are doing it and are enjoying every minute. What I learnt from them is that life is too short not to enjoy every minute of it. Why wait for everything to be perfect before you move into your dream house? Everything takes time and patience. Everything costs money and doing things yourself makes you appreciate it so much more. You can count on your friends to help you with anything in life. Even when you think that they might not want to help, ask them anyway. You will be surprised.

One of the adventures we had together was river rafting on the Orange River with four friends. I would never have thought that I would be able to do the rafting, but my friend assured us that we would do very little rowing. We would drift with the stream. Or so we thought. The first bit of the rafting was indeed drifting but in the last kilometre or two the wind started blowing from the front and we had to start rowing. This was in the middle of December and it was blisteringly hot. We were three per boat and we rowed and rowed until it felt as if the boat was standing still. I got very tired. Aimee and I started screaming at each other because she would say that I wasn't rowing hard enough and I would say that she wasn't rowing hard enough. We got so angry with each other that my friend thought at one point that we were going to hit each other with the oars. I'm happy to say we didn't though.

My friend had to get out of the boat and started pushing it for us because we just couldn't row anymore. At every corner she would say that the end was around the next corner. When we got to that corner she would say, 'Not this corner- the next one.' It felt as if we were rowing for days. We eventually reached the shore of where we were going to camp for the night before continuing with our next day's rowing trip. I was hot and red in the face from exhaustion. As we got to the top of the dam wall in the middle of nowhere, there was a cooler bag waiting. In the cooler bag was ice cold Beer. I haven't been that happy to see an ice cold beer in my entire life! I took the beer and tried to find a tree to sit under but there were no trees, only bushes. I went and lay down under a bush in a foetal position. Drinking my beer and eating my hot dog, sunburnt and *very* tired. The wind was blowing loudly and the air was dry. We had to go down to the shore of the dam to move out of the dust and sun. I was drinking whisky from a can. I was trying to feel better and the alcohol helped.

As the wind was still blowing a lot of sand into my face, sand ended up in my drinking can. I didn't realise that I was drinking sand until the middle of the night when my stomach wanted to work. It was a horrible feeling. I wanted to go outside to do my thing but there was a lot of movement outside the tent. I was sure that there were baboons out there and I didn't want to face them as baboons can be dangerous if they are surprised. So I filled my head with happy thoughts and waited patiently for the sun to rise. The sun just poking its' head out over the top of the mountain when I zipped open the tent and ran out, looking for a comfortable spot to do what I needed to. As I was walking around the bushes searching for the perfect spot, I realised that I had to dig a hole in the ground first before I could do anything. By now I had already been waiting for five hours to release the pressure in my stomach. I dug a hole in the ground and could at last do my thing. I was so relieved.

As we were breaking down the tents and getting ready to move on, Aimee saw a yellow spider in the corner of the tent. She screamed and was not happy. She told us that it had taken her an hour the previous night to close all the holes in the tent with plasters she had taken from the first aid kid. Desperate measures for desperate times. The tent looked like it had come out of a war zone with it being full of plaster patches. She thought that we would be safe from creepy crawlies if she did that. Clearly it did not work.

I was telling my friends how I'd had to wait for the sun to rise before I could go do my thing and they started laughing. I asked them why they were laughing and Anna said that they were the baboons. The noises I heard had been them walking around the tents looking for space to do *their* thing. I wasn't very impressed but I did learn a lesson that night. Rather look and see what is outside, before assuming that you are hearing baboons.

My friends said that they had never seen anyone bathing in a bowl of water as I had done the previous night. I had washed myself using three cups of water. They said that although there was very little water, it looked as if I'd had a shower. I laughed and said that I'd felt very dirty and had to clean myself.

We continued day two rowing/floating journey down the Orange River. We made it to the end and we had great fun in the process. I will never forget that journey doing something I had thought that I would never be able to do. I did it and think that I will do it again. But I might need to be rowing fit the next time.

Friends play a vital role in our lives. We need to treasure them. We need to have fun, be silly and play together. As adults we forget how to play as we get so caught up in our professional lives. Play like a child, you will see how you smile automatically when you start to explore. Don't just babysit your children, raise them.

Chapter Eleven

Vulnerability

I made the decision to accept what had happened in my teenage years and what I had done during that time of my life was a learning process and that it was important for me to learn from the things I had done. I know that my dad learnt valuable lessons, although it is very hard for him to remember some of the things that he did. One thing he always did when he woke up the day after a drinking binge with a hangover that would kill an average drinker, was to call me and apologise. There were times when I said horrible things to him, things that were hurtful and very personal. One day I apologised to him for something I had said to him and he looked at me and said, 'It takes a big man to make an apology, but it takes a bigger man to accept it.'

What I know now is that we are all vulnerable to society and in life. We want to be in control of everything and the moment we lose control, we become vulnerable. We think that by drinking we will numb our emotions but what we forget is that we are not just numbing the negative emotions; we are also numbing the positive emotions. Drinking causes the body and mind to react in a way that makes an individual feel in control. People think that it can act as a coping mechanism, but it actually just creates more depression. When you have had too much to drink, you wake up the next morning feeling even worse than you did before you had a drink. Depression kicks in because you feel nauseous, you have a massive headache and your stomach is upset. For that day you add no value at work or in society. You try to get up, but your headache is killing you. You try to eat but when you look at food, you want to throw up. You feel vulnerable to the extent of never wanting to get out of bed again. Some people will lie down and sleep it off; others will get up and start drinking again.

At a very young age these were the values and habits that I saw in people around me. At the age of 14 I thought that this was the way to act and react when times get tough. I had my first beer at the age 14 and, to be honest, I never looked back. I partied hard whenever I had the opportunity to. I became the person who would say, 'Life is messy, live with it.'

Throughout my schooling, my academic studies and my twenties, I consumed a lot of alcohol. I wanted to be accepted by the world that was presented to me in what I thought was the right way. Everyone else was doing it, so I must do it too. I knew then that I had muscular dystrophy and I knew that I was gay. I knew that I had gone to boarding school at the age of six. I knew that my dad had a drinking problem and I just wanted to be normal like everyone else. Drinking looked normal to me. Drinking and driving, spending all your money on alcohol, forgetting most of the people you met when you were drunk—those all became the norm for me.

At first I only drank on Fridays and Saturdays. Then it also became Wednesdays – which we used to call 'little Friday'. Then we started drinking on Thursdays - 'Phuza Thursdays.' (Phuza means drink). We would get so drunk over the weekend that our hangovers only started clearing by Tuesday or Wednesday. Your body would be sore, your liver and kidneys would feel as if you had lower back pain, you were thirsty all the time and longing for another drink to make you feel better. Another drink would numb the pain. You thought that you only had a personality when you'd had something to drink. That first glass of wine would make you socially acceptable again.

Fifteen years later I made the decision to stop being a binge drinker and then wanted to understand why life is so messy. I wanted to change my thinking from 'life is messy, live with it' to 'life is messy, -clear it up.' I started to understand that life is all about connection. We want to feel loved and valued as that gives us purpose and meaning. The ability to feel connected to others is the reason why we are here. When you ask people about connection, they tell you about disconnection. When you ask them about love, they tell you about heartbreak.

I realised that I had begun to feel ashamed of being disconnected. I felt that I wasn't good enough. There were things that I did not want to talk about or for people to know about. I started feeling shame and this created fear of feeling connected. I became really vulnerable.

I really wanted to fit in and I realised that I had a huge need to be loved and for belonging. I really wanted to feel worthy so I started to change my life around. I realised that life is special and we only have one life to live. The only person who can make you feel worthy is you when you really whole-heartedly want to. I started developing the courage to start living my life to my own rules. I started running my own race at my own pace. I had the courage to realise that I'm not perfect. I started having the compassion to be kind first to myself and then to others. I realised that I would never be able to treat others kindly if I cannot treat myself kindly. This is when I learnt about authenticity.

I was willing to let go of how the world had made me think I should be. I started to embrace vulnerability. What made me vulnerable made me beautiful. Vulnerability was necessary in my life. I started to become the person who wanted to say, 'I love you' first. I started to invest in a relationship that may or may not work out. I realised that cannot control and predict who I will become, but that I am able to allow myself to show compassion and to be vulnerable. I had to allow myself to be seen for who I really am.

At the beginning, the more I tried to understand or accept vulnerability, the more I pulled back. I tried to numb vulnerability with alcohol and drinking pain medication. What we need to understand is that we do not only numb vulnerability, shame and fear. At the same time we numb joy, gratitude and happiness. We first need to understand why and how we numb ourselves. We try and make everything that is uncertain, certain. Religion went from, 'I believe in faith' to 'I'm right, you're wrong, shut up.' The more vulnerable we are, the more we fear. We try and perfect everything.

We take fat from our butts and inject it into our cheeks[3]. We pretend that what we do and say does not have an effect on people. We need to let ourselves be seen, deeply seen, to love with our whole hearts. We need to practise gratitude and joy. We need to realise that: 'I am enough.' We need to stop screaming and to start listening. We are then kinder to others and kinder to ourselves. (Brene Brown)

---

[3] https://www.google.com/
Brené Brown on Vulnerability –TED Talk

Chapter Twelve

No Rules

I have experienced many different scenarios in my career and have learnt valuable lessons from every situation. In some situations, people do the weirdest things and I sometimes think to myself; 'Is that really possible?' I'm a strong believer that people see rules as something that need to be broken. I mean, it took me 12 years to finally realise that I'd broken more rules in my life than the number of complaints that I've dealt with. And I can assure you that I've dealt with *many* complaints in my working career.

When I was at school, the rules were simple. Your nails must be short. How short? Each girl's perception of 'short nails' differed. Back then I would strive to break the rules and, while I did not wear false nails, my nails were always longer than the school saw as 'normal length.' 14 years later I get irritated if my nails are even showing white tips as they get dirty quickly and managing long nails is just a hassle. It's so much easier to have short, neat nails or should I say that my perspective and my normal are now different. Back then it was not about my nails being long, it was more about breaking the rules. If the rule stated that you should not wear gel in your hair, I would wear gel in my hair. A teacher once asked me, 'Why is there gel in your hair?' I told her very politely that it was not gel, but mousse. If the rule stated that your dress must be four fingers above your knee, my dress would be shorter than that. That is where the saying, 'Rules are made to be broken' comes from. What would the world be like if there were no rules in schools, organisations and companies? Would it be successful, or would it be complete chaos?

While working in the health and wellness industry, this has always been a question on my mind. When I started at the company in 2001, the rules and regulation booklet consisted of 88 rules and I had to know every one of them. Currently (2016) we are on 170 rules, with more still being added. Every year the rule book changes and a new rule gets added when someone does something that is not acceptable in our facilities. Once that rule has been added, people will then find something else to do that is not acceptable. Where will it end?

Will people ever stop pushing the boundaries? To me it feels as if people do weird things just to get into trouble. Consider what I say in the context of having an affair. Is the affair really about finding the other person attractive or is it about doing something that is not right behind someone's back. Or is it about the sex?

Is it a rush to break your wedding vows? Vows are like rules which are there so that people know what is wrong and what is right, what you can and can't do. It is very difficult for humans to just be acceptable, everyone has different concepts of right and wrong.

When you tried smoking when you were not legally allowed to, did you do it because you like the rush of nicotine? Or did you do it for the rush of doing something illegal? People break rules and laws for different reasons. Every individual makes a choice to do or to act in a certain way and this can be to make them feel better about their life. Or they might be stealing from others to feed their family. It could also be just because they want to do something different. Whatever reasons people have for breaking rules or the law, might be frustrating to others or even have a negative effect on their lives. But for the people doing things they know are wrong, their behaviour is normal to them. To them, what they are doing is perfectly fine.

There are three things you can do about this:

- You can get upset and let the behaviour and choices of other people rule your life;
- You can smile about it and understand that people are different; or
- You can act or find ways to control the situations differently. Whatever makes you happy and positive, to enable you to stay sane.

The campaign for 'Time to End the War on Drugs' is a good example of people who were doing what they feel is right to them. The more government and the police tried to control drugs, the more out of control the situation got. Dealers started to go underground and the illegal use of drugs grew. The addicts picked up more drug-related illnesses and more addicts died because of taking their drugs in dark and lonely places where there is no help and no one cares. Society was not treating the patients, they were creating addicts. The argument was that the fear of prison drove addicts underground and that incarceration is far more expensive than treatment. When Portugal stopped their war on drugs, there was a decline in illegal drug use among teens and rates of new HIV infections caused by sharing needles dropped. At the same time, the number of people seeking treatment for drug addiction more than doubled. This is a clear indication that if you treat people like people, the chance that they will want to change is good.

Having no rules or laws would most probably create a world of chaos and uncertainty. People would need to be more responsible and socially acceptable if there were no rules or laws. We would probably have fewer members in our industry because of people doing whatever they liked. There would probably be more deaths, violence and misconduct too.

Would crime increase if there were no laws or rules?

I can sometimes just laugh at the excuses people can come up with when you ask them to pack away or not drop their weights. The most popular excuse is, 'The weights are heavy and have to be dropped' and, 'The reason why I don't pack away my weights is because I'm tired after I've done all my sets.'

I will then look at the person and asked them a polite question, 'Do you think that if you use lighter weights and do more sets, you might create a win-win situation for both of us?'

What people don't understand is that when they drop their weights, it is annoying to other members. It is also intimidating for women when a man drops a heavy weight right next to her. She might well never return to the weight section again! The weights are damaged when you drop them and when the weights are sent in for repairs; who is the first person to complain that they are not available? The person who drops the weights is usually the first to complain. Dropping weights poses a huge health and safety risk as you have no control over the weight if you just leave it to bounce. Pack away the weights after you have used them, leave the gym floor as clean as you would leave your mother's kitchen, be considerate and understand that there are many different cultures, races, genders and religions.

A member once lost his finger tip in the free weight section because he had too many weights lying around his bench while doing chest presses. He had to use three different weight sizes for his sets and instead of replacing the dumbbells each time, he left them lying on the floor. As he was putting one dumbbell down to rest, his finger got caught between the dumbbell in his hand and the dumbbell on the floor. It amputated his finger tip as the dumbbell weighed 40kg. We had to put the fingertip in a bag of ice and send it to hospital with the member.

For years the Super Circuit in the health and wellness industry was designed and managed as follows: you had to start at the number one station and go around the circuit until you reach the last one. Every time the lights beep, you need to change exercises and either move to the next machine or run on the steps. There are set rules that you need to obey for the circuit to run smoothly for everyone. If I tell you that the circuit area is the area in the health club industry that has the most incidents, you would probably say, 'How is that possible? There are set rules, people just have to follow them.' Yet it is because of the rules that people differ and attack each other verbally on the circuit. When I say verbally, I mean verbal abuse including swearing, racist remarks, and religious insults and really going into people's personalities and cultures. Unfortunately I'm not allowed to write about any specific incidents so all I can say here is that people are vicious creatures and that their words can get them into a lot of trouble. The people who make the remarks have no idea what impact their words have on the other person.

I had to come up with a solution for this ongoing problem and my innovation is the following: when we had a strength equipment refresher, I made the decision to take away all the rules and to change the name of the Super Circuit to a Free Zone. I removed all the lights and the numbers on the equipment. The new equipment had its own rep counters and I installed a digital clock so that people can still time themselves when they do their exercises. Personal trainers, members and whoever wants to use the area can now use it whenever they want to. No rules.

We have not had one incident in the Free Zone since we removed the rules. Members who were unhappy with the circuit rules having been removed, were helped in a different way. We would ask them what other routines they would do in the gym facility. Most of these people would say that the Super Circuit is the only exercise they want to do. We would then give them alternatives and assist them in working out a new program. The feedback we got was amazing and the members would come back and say that they could feel a real difference in their bodies, that they were losing more weight or building more muscle. They couldn't believe that they had only done the Super Circuit for years and had not realised that there is such a variety of exercises that one can do. The moral of this story is that rules can create conflict. When people do the same thing over and over, they will get the same result over and over. If you bring in change, people will react to it because it is different from their normal routine. If you help people and show them different ways of doing things, you can change the industry and people's lives for the better. Go on, do something different today. Challenge your normal and lift your boundaries to be different.

There are laws that tell us not to drink and drive but people are still not listening or obeying the law. There are still drunk drivers who kill scary numbers of innocent people on our roads every year. 'Don't drink and drive campaigns' are run every year but hundreds of people still die on the roads as a result of people not taking responsibility. How can we as a fitness industry expect people to obey the rules and regulations of our facilities, when they cannot obey to the laws of the country?

Rules and laws are created to protect people. To keep people safe and to create an environment that will be acceptable for everyone yet people still do whatever *they* think is right.

I would recommend that the company take away all the rules and implement only the following two:

- *Treat others the way you want to be treated.*
- *Leave everything and everyone better than you found them.*

Handling incidents and crisis situations is part of our job description. Incidents can be anything from theft, abuse, property damage or death. My worst fear is to experience a fatality in the facility as anyone can have a heart attack, stroke or some sort of medical emergency at any time. I thought that it would never happen to me.

Been there, done that, got the T-shirt. ***With regard to depression and stress, I always say, 'If everything is going well, you need to become scared. When people don't complain or talk about your business constantly, you are doing something wrong.' If you can see every complaint as a way of improving your business, you are on the right path. Take feedback and make it constructive and positive. Give people something before they even know they want it. You get good stress and bad stress. It is how you filter the stress that is important. Most people take every negative comment or business complaint very personally. They don't know a professional or more effective way in which to deal with the negative comment or feedback.***

The reason for this is that people work hard. Our parents told us to work hard as it's the only way to make money. Without money you will not be successful, without success you will be poor.

What happens to most people today?

They work hard with long hours and little downtime. They drain themselves emotionally and physically until they break down.

Leverage stress as an advantage. Stress is a valuable tool as it pushes you to get out onto your edges. Stress is where growth and mastery live. The key is to recover from stress afterwards.

Why do we work hard, why not rather work smart?

We imitate what we know and see. My dad used to work very hard on the farm and my mom is a housewife who still works very hard. Neither of them has a lazy hair on their heads. We did have growing pains in our relationship while I was growing up but I still learnt valuable lessons from them and my culture was established as a little girl. Combine working hard and working smart and you will have a winning combination.

What has happened to the youth of this century, why are they not playing or being creative? Most children today spend most of their days in front of the TV. The children know more about technology than I do and this makes me both scared and uncomfortable. I realised that the universe has changed immensely and evolution seems to have made the kiddies super humans. I did not have the opportunity to do what they do today when I was a kid. Not that I would have wanted to, but I do admire them.

I will never change what I had as a child for anything. And I really don't think that today's children, locked into virtual worlds of TV and games have a better childhood than my brother and I had playing our games outside on the farm. I can catch up with technology if I want but I am not really motivated to. I like being the way I am. I'm very practical and innovative and the universe needs a mix of everything. If we can just find ways to balance everything, life would be so easy. Or so I think.

Life is as easy or difficult as you make it. If you want complicated, you will get complicated. If you want simple, you will get simple. As adults we forget how to play like kids. What I mean by this is that we want to be the adults and thus want to control everything.

When last did you just 'play'? Parents don't play with their kids anymore but instead pay money to other people and organisations to play with them. Most parents don't have time to play with their kiddies as both parents have to work to make a living. Life has become a race to either save time or to create more time. The one thing in life you can't buy is time.

Parents will call playing with their kiddies, having Fun.

Sport stars will call playing sport, having Fun.

We get taught by life coaches to love your work and to have Fun.

Company values include the word Fun.

We call playing having fun. Or think about what your idea of fun is?

For a long time in my life I thought that drinking and partying was fun. I got stuck in thinking like that for most of my twenties and it made me busy, busy doing nothing of value. Most of the time I filled my weekends with useless conversations and headaches and I can hardly remember some conversations I had during that time. My life was, and still, is a roller-coaster ride.

Use your imagination. Create your perfect world. See the goals that you want to achieve. Create mental maps of what you want achieve in life by thinking creatively. You can achieve wonderful things through your thinking.

My brother always had ways of making life fun and he was full of ideas. One day he took toothpicks and stuck them into the hallway carpet in an upright position. The red carpet became a battlefield of tooth picks and he would then chase me around in the house and tickle me until I wet myself from laughing and started crying. Then my dad would come running down the hallway to see what was happening. The trap of toothpicks was waiting for him to step on and then he would not be able to give my brother a hiding. That had been the whole plan, according to my brother. However, he made one mistake and my dad was a step ahead of him. He would chase my brother as if they were playing and he would run around and laugh as if they were having so much fun. My brother became so distracted that he forgot all about his own toothpick minefield and ran straight into it. Crying and pulling tooth picks from his feet, he had fallen into his own trap. He was defeated by my dad and I got my revenge.

Without lifting a hand, my dad had ways to get lessons that he wanted us to learn through to us. What I learnt from him was to be innovative, don't break other people down to achieve your end result, plan carefully. You always need help to execute a perfect plan and in life what you give, you will receive. The world has a way of showing you what you are doing wrong or what you need to do to learn a valuable lesson. Without making mistakes or trying something new, you will never know what the outcome could be if you don't try it. If you fail, it is about how quickly you get up again. Learn from your mistakes.

Have fun, be silly and play like a child sometimes. It will awaken the child in you. It will make you feel relaxed or uncomfortable. If you wonder why it makes you feel uncomfortable, it is because you are not in control. You have let go of the control and if you can do that, you will start living. You will start seeing the beauty in life.

Chapter Thirteen

Behind the White Screens

It was the beginning of January 2006 and I had just finished work and gone for an exercise session. While I was training, I saw the members and staff become panicked and I looked over the edge to the swimming pool. As I walked down the stairs, I saw that there was a man lying on the edge of the pool and a woman sitting next to him. The manager on duty and a fitness instructor were both standing next to him. Many people were surrounding the man, but no one is actually doing anything so I ran to the pool to assist. When I got to the man, he had already turned blue in the face. I cleared the area of unnecessary people and obstructions. I tried to do chest compressions but the man was too big and I was too weak. Another member came to assist and I instructed him on how to do the compressions. He got it right, or so I thought. I tried to give air to the man as he was not breathing. His wife was holding his head, she was shaking with fear and the man's head was moving with her shaking hands so it became very difficult for me to do the breaths efficiently. His wife was screaming and crying, 'Please don't die on me today!'

I had to get someone to remove the wife from her dying husband. As I tried to open his mouth to insert the mouthpiece, I wasn't able to open it to get air in, it was as if his teeth had locked. The man's son was also standing next to his body, calling his name, crying and asking his dad to wake up.

It was really hard for me to stay calm; I was shaking and my mouth was dry. If I have to express what my emotions on that day were, I only have one word, 'Scared.' I was kneeling, trying my best to save a man's life. We kept up the CPR for 15 minutes until a doctor arrived on the scene and pronounced the man dead. For 15 minutes I breathed for a man who had already passed away. It was the worst experience of my life. I can still see the man's face in front of me, I can still remember how his eyes looked and how his stomach swelled from the air I was blowing into him. I can remember that I wanted to connect the Automatic External Defibrillator (AED) machine onto his body but I couldn't connect it in a wet area. We wanted to move the man but his wife did not want us to move him.

As I stood up, my knees were aching and my feet felt dead. I looked at the boy and his mother and saw the devastation on their faces. I did not know what to say or do. I was speechless, heartbroken and distracted. As I tried to get control of my emotions, I saw the doctor put a blanket over the man. As I looked around, I saw people staring and taking photos of the dead man. I became furious and the General Manager gave the instruction to evacuate the building. People were upset when we cleared the building and asked why they had to leave. They wanted to keep on training in the areas where they couldn't see the body. People showed no respect or feeling towards the man lying under the blanket, dead by the pool with his wife and child crying next to him. They wanted to finish their routine exercise session first before leaving. Some people wanted to take a photo to show someone else, maybe post it on Social media or make a video of, 'How to die in a Gym.' and load it on social media. There were even people taking pictures of the crying woman and child through the window of the swimming pool.

We are becoming a nation of cell phone cowards, legions of do-nothing mobile Phone creeps who think that helping a fellow man or woman begins and ends with pressing 'record.' There used to be a time in our lives when we would rush to another's aid. Now we're more likely to rush to capture someone's distress, just for a chance at a snippet of YouTube fame. The more the staff tried to clear the area, the more it felt as if most of the people were just ignoring us. People are different and some respectfully left the building immediately when the incident happened. Not all people know how to handle emergency situations or how to deal with scenarios where death is involved. What I must mention is that you should not monopolise the phone line when people need to contact the emergency services in the case of an assault, car accident or violence. If you are not phoning the police, ambulance or fire brigade, you are preventing someone else from doing so. After the chaos subsided, I had to sit down and write an incident report. Because I was so stressed, it was very difficult for me to recall the entire incident.

The next day, the staff received trauma counselling and I told the counsellor that I felt helpless and incompetent. A man had died while I was trying to save his life; I blamed myself for not saving him. My inadequacy led to a wife and boy being without a husband and father for the rest of their lives. For months I tried to figure out whether I could have done anything different. I played the entire incident over in my mind from start to finish, trying to fix the past. I realised after many months that the man was dead and that my trying to change the reality was not going to bring him back. The man's wife sadly also passed away after a long fight with cancer. The entire situation taught me life lessons that I will never forget. I make sure that all the staff members know what to do in the case of an emergency.

I tell this story in most of my training and development sessions to demonstrate that all the training and medical drills in the world cannot prepare you for the real incident. It helps with the process of getting everything done, but the emotional part of the incident takes many months to heal and never goes away entirely. That is what I learnt after the second heart attack, seven years later. To this day, on January 5th of every year, I dream about the swimming pool and I still have nightmares about the incident.

I was at home in bed reading a book when I received the call. My assistant was on duty at the time of the incident and when she phoned me, she sounded distressed and panicky. I told her to breathe and to make sure that all processes were in place. Her voice sounded as if she wanted to start crying.

'A man had a heart attack on the squash court. He is still alive and the paramedics are on site busy resuscitating him.' she said. I tried to calm her down but realised that she needed me. Within five minutes I was at the facility. I tried to run up the stairs but had torn my toe ligaments, so it was hard for me to walk. As I got up the stairs, I saw the man lying on the floor with the white screens around him. I looked to my left and saw his wife and daughter sitting a few feet away. I took over from my assistant and tried to comfort the wife and daughter although I did not know what to say. I saw that the man's chest had already turned blue from the compressions and I saw how they shocked him with the AED, they struggled to find a pulse. At that stage, I could not tell the lady that everything was going to be fine as I knew that there might be a chance that the man would not make it. As I looked around, I saw people trying to look around the screens at what was happening. I immediately walked up to them and asked them to move away. I asked how they would feel if it was their father or husband lying on the floor fighting for his life.

I saw the faces of the staff and realised how shocked they were. The one fitness instructor was pale and I could see that he was devastated. His face and entire body showed that he was not coping. I called him and asked him to keep the members away from the scene. The man's wife was shaking and in visible shock. I told them to stay where they were and that it was not a good idea to look at him in that state. If he died, it would be important to remember him as he had been. No one would want to watch their husband die.

The man gasped for air and this was the cue for the paramedics to take him to hospital. As he left the club, the people who had been involved in the incident were in shock. About 10 minutes after the man was taken to hospital, the paramedic phoned to inform us that he had passed away. I had to give the message to the fitness instructor who had given him CPR. As I gave him the message, he started crying. I ran my hand across his forehead and told him that he had done everything in his power to save the man's life. I sat down with them until they looked as if they could go home. It was late in the evening and we sat in dead silence for some time. Looking down at the floor, we slowly walked home.

When I got home that evening, I got straight into bed but as I tried to fall asleep, images of the man started running through my mind. All the memories of the previous incident started to flash through my mind again as well. I could clearly feel, see and hear what had happened at that time too. I took a sleeping pill and a fell asleep but I woke up in the middle of the night, not knowing what day it was or what had happened. I'd had a horrible dream; I dreamt about everything that had happened. I said to myself that it doesn't matter how much you want to forget the past, it always somehow finds a way back into your mind.

The next day I sat with the people who'd been involved in the incident. As I spoke to them, I realised that nothing had prepared them for this. They had done everything perfectly and according to our policies and procedures but nothing could have prepared them for the emotional part. As I listened to each of them, I started crying. I could feel their devastation and emotions and related to the pain they were feeling. One guy told me that he had never thought that the stories I told in training were true and had definitely thought something like that would happen to him.

Two nights before this incident happened, I'd had a weird feeling that something bad was going to happen. I posted a message to my heads of departments on our social media group and told them to be careful and alert. That night I left work to go home, my assistant's last words to me were, 'I hope tonight is quiet and that there is no drama.' She got what she was thinking about and I got what I dreaded. *The power of our thinking is extreme. What we think, will happen, will happen to us. It is important to control your thoughts.* My assistant said afterwards that we had 'jinxed' her with our thoughts. It could be true. Before you go to work, you have to tell yourself that it is going to be a great shift and you are going to have fun. That everything will be great. Then everything will be great. If you think negative thoughts, negative things will happen.

It takes time to get over major incidents like this. We are not doctors or paramedics who work with these situations every day so we get emotionally scarred for life. We blame ourselves and feel incompetent if we fail to save a life. As General Managers, we listen to and counsel the people involved in incidents like this one. I recalled previous incidents when this sort of thing had happened as I spoke to them and told them that we are human and it was fine to feel the way they did. 'As long as you know you did everything in your power to save the person's life, you have nothing to feel bad about,' I told them...

The next incident I'm going to write about was the day when I almost lost my job. It was 18h00 when I left the facility to go home for the day. As I got home and put my handbag down, my phone rang. It was the manager on duty and she tried to sound calm and collected, but what I heard was a frantic and terrified voice.

'Siekie, a weight fell from the second floor onto a kid's head in the pool,' she said. My first thought was, 'How the hell is that possible?' She then informed me that the paramedics were already on site and that the situation was under control. Although I trust my staff members, I put my shoes back on and rushed back to the club. There was blood everywhere on the pool deck and we had to close the pool to clean up the area and to get the pool safe again.

I started my investigation to determine what had happened. As I looked at the CCTV footage, I was amazed at what I was seeing. As the little girl made a tumble turn, the 10kg weight plate dropped from the second floor onto her head. There was no one in sight in the area where the plate dropped from. If the girl had swum one second slower or faster, the plate would have missed her. It was horrible to watch the impact of the weight on her head. Her head tilted forward and the water prevented her neck from snapping. She had a bun in her hair underneath her swim cap and that stopped the 10kg weight from cracking her skull open. From what I saw on the CCTV footage, the girl should have died at the point of impact. She was very lucky that day as her bun saved her life. She received 12 stiches and had whiplash but after two weeks she was swimming again.

It was very hard for me to speak to the child's parents and I couldn't find the right words to describe to them that a 10kg weight plate had fell from the top floor onto their daughter's head. We were almost responsible for their child's death. As I explained to her mother that the plate had fallen but that there was no one close to the rail or the plate, it felt weird. It did not sound right at all but the accident was a fluke. I wanted to blame someone or something but ultimately, I was accountable. The parents were very understanding and we had and still have a great relationship. The only request they had was that we make the top floor safe from weights falling to prevent this type of incident from happening again.

This incident forced the company to spend thousands of rands on making 108 Gyms safe from this type of thing happening again. We determined later that because of the free weights floor being a suspension floor, all the heavy weight movement caused the 10kg plate too slowly but surely move forward. This is one reason why it is crucial that members pack their weights away after using them.

The company is very good with running reports and stats on everything relevant. One year we had zero fatalities in our region for the entire year and also saved four lives as a region. On the first day of the next year, just after 07h00, a man had a heart attack in one of our regions clubs and passed away. We can go one whole year without a fatality and with saving lives and then on the other hand, you can start a year with a fatality.

Incidents happen all the time and we even have a saying in our industry that October and January are high risk incident months. The reason for this is that in October people come back to our facilities after the winter, after eating cake and drinking hot chocolate and not making any attempt to go to gym during the winter months. When they hit the gym on the first day back, they think they are as fit as they were five months before. Their body immediately goes into shock and they either get injured, or they have a heart attack. The same happens in January when people have overeaten and drunk too much during the December holidays. January comes and the entire country has New Year's resolutions. As General Managers, we start to prepare ourselves mentally weeks before January when our facilities are jam-packed and the incident stats are high. We prepare our staff to be mentally and emotionally prepared for aggressive members. We prepare them for medical incidents. We prepare them for racial attacks, member complaints and just plain straightforward impatient, rude and inconsiderate people. As General Managers, we go on our knees every morning and ask God to give us the strength to get through the day. 'Please God, help me today and give me the strength to understand why people can be so unreasonable, ugly and rude. Help me to stay calm, patient and to treat everyone with respect.' Then you get up and you go to work.

What keeps us going is the one good comment or the one life that was saved. We have saved many lives in our industry although you will never read about those in the media. Most of the time you will only read and know about the bad incidents.

In the evenings when you get home, you fall down into a chair and stare emotionlessly at the TV screen. You got to work at 08h00 and you only left at 19h00. Your partner, wife or husband will ask you how your day was - you will just say, 'It was okay.' They will ask you questions and tell you about their day but you will hear nothing. For 12 hours you either listened to complaints or you had to counsel staff members who needed your help because someone called them incompetent or racist. You will eat your food, but you will not taste what you are busy eating. You just eat, because you have to eat. When somebody actually asks you the next day if you slept well or what you had for dinner last night, you can't remember. Your mind was so busy processing your day that you did not even think about what you were eating. Your life becomes so busy and rushed that you do not even taste your coffee. You drink coffee, but you don't taste it. You go on your knees again to close off the day. 'Thank you God for giving me the strength to survive another day.'

Chapter Fourteen

One Nation, One Club

When you read the following stories, I'm sure they will make you ask, 'Does this *really* happen?'

I've written about rules in previous chapters and have mentioned on numerous occasions that rules are there to be broken. I want to add to that by saying, **'Rules are there to protect you. Rules are there to guide people to do "what is right". Or to do what is normal.'** Is that true?

"There are people cooking in the sauna.' At first I couldn't believe what I had just heard but I ran to the sauna. When I got there, a lady and her two children were sitting in the sauna looking at the sauna stove. To my amazement, I saw a rolled up piece of tin foil on the stove. Obviously it was extremely hot so I ran to get a towel to remove the foil from the sauna stones. As I opened the foil, I saw three eggs. As I was trying to explain to the lady that they are not allowed to do their cooking on the sauna stove, she just looked at me. 'No English – she responded.' I took her and her two children to the bench in the change room trying to explain that eating and cooking are not allowed in the sauna. After about an hour of explaining, I think they finally understood me. I never saw them in the sauna again.

The day I caught a 15 year-old trying to smoke in the steam room, was when I knew my job was going to be interesting. Common sense certainly does not seem to be common sense to everyone. I told the girl that if she wanted to smoke in hiding, she needed to do it in a place that is not filled with steam.

Imagine you are sitting in the steam room. You are used to talking to the people sitting with you and normally you would chat about the weather or that the steam room is too hot. Topic of the year in 2016 are the water restrictions and drought in South Africa. Or you would complain about work, even chat about your family or children. Imagine now that as you are chatting to the person sitting behind you, you hear them making strange noises, the type of noise you would hear when someone is getting some extreme sort of pleasure. You turn around and see a person, sitting with a towel around their body and wearing a swimming cap and goggles. Hearing the 'noise' should already have warned you that it is time to get out. The worst that could happen is you sitting naked, chatting your heart out when you realise that something is not right. You stand up, tell the person they are disgusting and then the person who responds – is a man! Yes, you will freak out. That is exactly what happened on one occasion.

This guy was clever. He would put on his swim suit; wrap his towel around his entire body, put on a swimming cap and go and sit in the ladies steam room. He would use the entrance from the pool side to get to the ladies steam room without being seen using the main entrance. What happened to the guy was inevitable; the poor lady never went into a steam room again without first talking to the person already sitting in there.

As we deal with these kinds of incidents, you might think they are clear cut. The people are wrong so they will either cancel their membership or accept their punishment. If that was what you were thinking, you are very wrong! People are never wrong; according to anyone involved in any type of incident in our gyms, they are never wrong. When my staff ask a person to please use a sweat towel, the member will respond by accusing them of being racist. When my people ask clients to obey to the 20 minute limit on cardio equipment or to remove their child from a treadmill – the member will start yelling at them and telling my people that they are paying their salaries. Members do this because they are either not sure about the rules or they are taking a chance, hoping we will not say anything. We remove children under the age of 14 from treadmills, not because we want to be difficult but because we want to protect them as it is not safe for a child to run on a treadmill. The things people say to the staff are just horrifying and members seem not to realise that the staff are just doing their jobs. When I do coaching or counselling sessions with my people, I remind them not to take the remarks from members personally. Members are angry at the rule, not at the person they take their frustration out on.

When serious incidents occur, we have to meet with all parties involved and get their statements and their sides of the story. When we have all the statements, we make a decision with the assistance of our legal department and Director. Doing the investigation and meeting with the different parties is difficult, but what is most terrifying is expelling, suspending or warning the person who was in the wrong. When you phone them to tell them about the outcome, they start screaming and shouting at you. Most often you will be accused of being a racist, inconsistent or biased. Even when you tell them that the decision is final, they will still tell you how incompetent and pathetic you are. You will be too scared to look at your Inbox, because you are scared to read about how they will sue you. I had one guy tell me that he would break my arms off. Another one spat on my table and said that he knows where I live.

I received a call from one of the General Managers one day. She said sarcastically, 'Siekie, we had a knife stabbing.' I had a grin on my face when I answered her, 'Tell me about it.' She started by telling me that two boys under 18 had gotten into a fight just outside the facility. As the one was bigger than the other, the small guy pulled out a knife and stabbed the other one three times in his back. There was blood all over the place. She said that there were just police and ambulances everywhere and it looked like a Christmas tree outside. She was calm but really afraid that it would become a big media story. When the media get involved with an incident, it usually gets completely out of hand. Nobody died on that day but there were serious consequences for the parties involved. Children do not understand the impact of their actions and that at such a young age they will have a police record for attempted murder and assault. The offender's entire working career will be affected.

We have had numerous water restriction problems over the past five years as water is getting very scarce in South Africa. One would think when the entire city is struggling with water pressure or just to have sufficient water supply, that people would understand when we do not have water. They don't. They expect us to have water. They will not have water at home, but when they go to the gym in the same area, they expect there to be water there, not realising that we are also just as dependant on the municipality to supply us with water as their homes are. In South Africa it is becoming very difficult to run a business and if we don't get sufficient water supply, we cannot fill our pools, flush our toilets or even supply sufficient showers. Sometimes we have no water or electricity at the same time which results in no air conditioning. In summer the temperature outside can rise up to 37 degrees. Imagine exercising with no water, no air con, and with 300 people in the same building in that heat!

As business managers we feel so powerless because we want to provide a service to our members, we want to fix things, but we are not able to. We can't send an email to God asking him to send us rain as rain would relieve the water supply problems. We have to depend on the government to assist businesses with water supply.

Businesses are losing money and some businesses are closing down as a result of insufficient supply of water and electricity. The unemployment rate is rising. When will the government realise that our beautiful country is going backwards?

The thing that hurts the most is when you have done everything in your power to make all your members happy; you work hard and listen to complaints all the time. I realised that you will never make everyone happy. Some people are rude, inconsiderate and sometimes just plain arrogant.

An elderly lady walked into my office. She was furious because another lady had been brushing her teeth in the basin. This lady said that it is disgusting to brush your teeth in a basin. In amazement I looked at her and asked, 'Ma'am, where do you brush your teeth?' She responded that she brushed her teeth in the shower and I responded by saying that for me, it is disgusting to brush your teeth in the shower. She did not like that very much but I pointed out to her that people are different. Some people's normal is to brush their teeth in a basin while other people brush their teeth in the shower. We need to understand that there are different cultures in South Africa. Our back grounds and values are different and we go about doing things differently.

The previously disadvantaged groups in our country mainly grew up in informal settlements. They did not have running or sufficient water supply and many people had to walk miles to get water from the nearest river or a communal tap. They would then carry the water to their homes in big buckets and pour it into a small bucket as big as a basin. With that little bit of water, the entire family would have to bath and wash themselves. For many years that was their normal. When apartheid faded away, the groups were introduced to better facilities. They were introduced to showers, baths and running water that is available when you open a tap. For them it was a challenge to change to the way other groups and cultures were already doing things. For Western cultures, it was not normal to see people washing and bathing in a basin, it was weird to them. Both groups need to adapt and to live with the normal of other cultures. We need to understand that people have different realities. What works and what is normal to you, is not normal to others.

If we can understand that we need to behave and be considerate of each individual's cultural needs, we would be able to achieve our goal as One Nation, one Club.

Chapter Fifteen

The Power of Great Leaders

To work for a Gym, you have to have the right DNA. You need to be an activist for the Gym brand and you need to truly believe in the values that Gym stands for. Every staff member needs to understand the purpose of the business and what we want to achieve. I've worked for and learnt many things from many great leaders in my career. The lady who appointed me in 2001 is still working for the Gym and for a period in my General Manager career, she was my Human Resources Manager. She taught me how to work with and understand people. She taught me to see things from the other person's perspective and to understand where some people are coming from. Every time we see each other, I just feel grateful and I have thanked her many times for believing in me and giving me the opportunity to work for such an amazing company. The company is constantly changing and trying out new and innovative products. Restructuring takes place in order to position the company better and to make leaders more responsible. Whenever you think that this is where you want to be or is the highest that you can go, another opportunity arises. The growth opportunities are endless as the company grows annually by developing new facilities worldwide.

You do not need a title to lead and can lead in any department, industry or company. A title does not give you the right to treat people differently. Quote from a wise person: 'With a title the responsibility becomes bigger.'

Fraxional Excellence is the smallest change/action which has the biggest effect (ripple effect). As stated by a director of Gym, JH, you must not focus on being brilliant, focus on being BETTER at everything you do and Brilliance will be the outcome. The 0.5% principle as explained by a doctor; the greatest wins and losses in sport almost always fall on either side of a 0.5% margin. How most games and races have been won by great sport stars is by them making a split second decision. In the 1995 Rugby World Cup final when South Africa played the All Blacks, on paper it was a definite win for the All Blacks. The purpose of a win for South Africa was not only that it was beneficial for the team, but for the whole country. The 1995 World Cup win united South Africans and made the Springboks want to win even more. The split second decision by the fly half to drop kick the ball resulted in a win for South Africa. Winners all have one thing in common, they understand, and more importantly believe in, their PURPOSE.

What impact does this philosophy have on any business?

We have key performance indicators that we have to achieve on a monthly basis. Every business has key performance indicators which they use to manage and track performance in their business. Every month we win or lose with a 0.5% margin either with sales, net promoter score or profit. The difference between winning and losing often boils down to that one day it didn't go your way or that one decision that cost you. It is that one day when you decide to go to work not because you want to but because you have to. You are at work, but you left your brain at home. In business it is essential that you go to work and give 110% every day. Not just when you feel like it, but every single day.

Your role is to understand that the principle does exist and to have the foresight to prepare your teams and practise the skills and disciplines needed to make that 0.5% decision when required. This is the concept of Fraxional Excellence. Focus on what people want as opposed to what you think they need. Find their PURPOSE. Do 100 things, 1% better as opposed to doing 1 thing 100% better.

We make a choice when we wake up in the morning. We choose to go to work and do what is expected of us. People often think that in the health and wellness industry you only have personal trainers and you exercise for the entire day. Little do people know that we lead and manage people. It is not just about keeping the facility clean and all the equipment in working order. It is not just dealing with complaints and making members happy; there is so much more to the business than just that.

We have some of the best leaders in our business. The health and wellness industry is a fast growing industry that is striving for excellence. The golden rule in our business is to treat others the way you want to be treated. If you get that principle right in your business, you will have happy customers, happy people and happy suppliers.

Learning from an exceptional leader is a real inspiration to me. I was always nervous when I heard that the MD was on his way to visit my region. I always put a lot of thinking into what he was going to ask. What would be the correct answer? Am I doing the right thing? Or, I hope that my people are not doing anything that could make my life difficult. I even did a web search of him to see what his last press release was about and what his planning around growing the business is. I don't think that any General Manager will ever be prepared to spend time with the MD.

On this specific day, I changed my approach around what and how the day would be. I decided to stop focussing on what we do wrong and started focussing on what we do right. I ended up learning so much from him that his visit inspired me to write about him.

He has a presence when he enters a room or when he speaks to people. He dresses to impress and loves to talk about the business and makes time for the people who work for him. He focuses on what and how our product can keep members engaged. He emphasises taking the time to employ the right people and spending time developing them to become great leaders and managers. He has a real passion for the business and for how to move the company forward. What I learnt from him is that trust is hard earned. It takes years to build trust and it can be broken in a heartbeat. He wants to trust all his General Managers and wants them to take responsibility and be accountable for their businesses. He said that the company will always employ the best person for the job irrespective of what your skin colour, age, gender or culture is. There are numerous learning and development programs for previously disadvantage groups to help them to get the correct leadership skills to enable them to move up in the business.

My passion is to develop people from cleaners to leaders. There are many examples in our business units of where we have developed people from cleaning floors and scrubbing toilets to becoming General Managers. It is the best feeling in the world when you have trained and developed a person and they become a leader. In some instances they even become better than you are. The company has a proactive approach when it comes to the development and appointment of people.

He asked me the following question:

'What is the difference between being clever and being wise?'

'I don't know, please tell me?'

He said that being clever is to know that a tomato is a fruit, to be wise is to know not to put the tomato in a fruit salad.

I got a smile on my face knowing that this great analogy is going to stick with me for the rest of my life. He showed so much wisdom and leadership that I felt humble in his presence. We spoke about everything; we covered politics, employment equity, financials, company growth and the city expansion.

He also said that a title does not mean anything. What goes with a title is that you get to work so much harder to earn peoples trust. In order for people to follow a leader, they need to feel that they are being led. He likes it when people are innovative and wants innovation to focus on what the main thing is. Keep the main thing, the main thing. Don't fiddle around with sales commission structure as sales people want to be in control of their own success so your commission structure needs to support that. Sales people will compete if they know that the goal is realistic, fair an achievable. Always have a good recruitment process. If you have a sales team of five, you need to turn one person every six months, preferably the weakest link in the team. This is to avoid complacency. See the potential in your current employees and grow them into sales people. This will generate constant healthy competition and it will create energy within the team.

You need to have a proper plan in place to prevent and control your bad debt. Cheap is not always the best way to go as people want to pay for value. Give them the value and they don't mind the price. Always know what your competitor is up to. Be present and know what their next step is going to be.

Another great leader in the health and wellness industry is JG. I have worked with him for many years and enjoyed every minute. He is the type of leader who listens to your suggestions and innovations. He allows you to run your business according to your own standards and he allows you to create your own business culture. He is not in the business to create little 'mini MEs'. In the business industry there are many leaders who like to create people who do things in the same way that they do. Doing that limits an individual from reaching their full potential.

JG is a person with emotional intelligence and he understand exactly what motivates each employee. It is fascinating to watch him do his 'thing'. He talks to many people in one day and he remembers details of each individual's personal and work life. You can share your stories with him as he is trust worthy and has high moral values.

JG has been in the company for many years and is an inspiration to all the employees. He started many years ago as a Fitness instructor, he moved through different departments to become what he is today, which is a Director. He worked in the following departments: personal trainer, reception, front of house manager, operations, assistant general manager and then General Manager. It took him three years to move from no title to becoming a manager. He was then appointed as a Cluster General Manager and in 2008 he became a leader as a Regional Business Manager. For 10 years, JG worked his butt off to become the leader he is today. The lesson to learn from this story is that it can take you 10 years to become a guru or a master at what you do. Be patient and work your butt off.

In any businesses you need a mentor and a coach and JG is my coach. All the great leaders in the world have coaches and mentors. The great Entrepreneurs of the world all have coaches as you cannot run a business effectively without having a coach. There are three things you never cut down on in business and they are marketing, branding and learning and development.

Learning and development has had a massive impact on the business. It created the opportunity for the company to identify more female leaders and this has allowed the company to empower women into leadership positions. 60% of the General Managers our industry in 2016 are women and this is a great statistic. What stands out is that the women in leadership positions get a salary equal to that the men earn.

JG is always willing to help and even when he has had very little sleep, he listens to you. When you make decisions, you can always count on him to have your back. In the business world it is essential to know that your leaders have your back. The company empowers their General Managers to make business decisions as long as those decisions have a positive impact on the member experience. By allowing them to make important decisions without approval, a mind-set of accountability amongst leaders in the business is created.

The health and wellness industry does things differently. They challenge the norm continuously with great innovation on product and people. The company also gives salary increases at the end of every April, not like most companies that do it in January or December. Be careful to change the salary increases if your business already has a structure. Due to a lack of understanding or their cultural background, changing your structure can result in people resigning by thinking that if you give them a salary increase only in April, the company owes them money from January to April. They will think that if you give the increase only in April, you screwed them over for the last four months. People think differently about salaries.

An example is when the company decided to increase the sales consultants' basic salary in January one year, I received many resignations and started interviewing the consultants to determine why they were resigning when they received an increase. In the interviews, people told me that for six months they had been at R400 less than they were now worth. They felt that the company owed them for the six months that were paid at the previous basic. I thought that they were crazy to think like that but in the end I realised that their reality is different to mine and the way they perceive the corporate industry is just their normal. The way they've been bought up is their normal, we cannot change that.

Be the entrepreneur of your business unit, take accountability for it and be real. Be open to suggestions and learn from the people around you. Be the best you can be, and then some more.

When you get to the end of your career or life, you have to think of how people will remember you. What legacy will you leave behind? Don't wish that you were happier, be happy today. People will be happy around you when you start with your own happiness. Don't wish that you didn't work so hard. Work smart and play to your strengths. Do the work that you are best at. Do the work that you were born to do.

Chapter Sixteen

The 10 Things I Now Know that I Wish I had Known on Day One

- *1. Never judge a book by its cover*

My journey with the Gym began as a part-time receptionist in December 2001. The day I went for the interview I was wearing shorts, a T-shirt and flip flops. The interview panel consisted of five people. I was scared and did not know what to expect.

'Is it really necessary to have an interview with so many people?' I thought.

Your thoughts would probably be, 'How difficult can an interview for a receptionist position be?'

I was a mere 20 years old and at that age it was a very difficult interview for me. During the interview I felt as if I couldn't breathe and black spots started appearing in front of my eyes. I thought I was going to faint.

All that went through my mind was that I should make eye contact with as many of the panel as possible. About halfway through the interview, I felt confused and no longer knew how to answer. I dropped my head onto the table and lay on my arms. When I looked up again after two seconds, I smiled and said to them, 'If you employ me, I promise that I will work hard and become the best at what I do.'

The two things I learnt that day were to never judge a book by its cover and to make people feel comfortable when they come for interviews. I got my first real job! I felt very relieved and happy and made a promise to myself that I would make the best of being a receptionist.

- *2. Don't be a clock watcher*

While working as a receptionist at the Gym, I was also busy doing my degree in Human Movement Science. It was very important to me to get higher education. In my year overseas I had worked really hard to save for a financial foundation to start my studies. As a student, I had to make a living and look after myself. ***It's not a good idea to create too much debt when you are a student; remember that you will have to pay that debt off for many years to come.*** The Gym is very close to my heart as the company has done a lot for me over the years. I've worked with amazing people and learnt how to take control of my life. The day I started working there, I had no idea how big the brand was. To be honest though, the brand was fairly new to South Africa at that stage.

When I began my job, my dad taught me an important lesson. He asked me if I wanted to be rich. My obvious response was, 'Of course I want to be rich. Who does not want to be rich?'

He replied, 'Your success in becoming rich will be your choice. If you work from 08h00 to 17h00 and are a clock watcher, you will never be rich. Rich people work from early in the mornings until the job is done. They not only work hard, they also work smart. Start your journey at your job but remember to never be lazy. Sometimes you will need to give before you can receive.'

Those wise words have stayed with me. Whenever I need to make a big decision, I always refer back to my dad's advice. As a farmer, he had to work 24 hour days.

My first salary was R980 a month. At that stage of my life, that was a lot of money. When I saw the money in my bank account, I went, 'WOW this is a lot of money, I can do a lot with this money!' I was really happy and used my money wisely. Or so I thought. Three months down the line, I realised that the R980 was not enough money for me; I needed to earn more. I then started coaching hockey at my previous school and coached the U/16 D and C girl's hockey teams. I was paid R800 for the term coaching hockey. Just for the record, both of my teams won their respective leagues that year.

I also worked at a physiotherapist for a few hours in the afternoons. I helped with rehabilitation of clients with different injuries and for that I got paid R10 an hour. I worked really hard and also worked long hours. I studied full time at university and worked three jobs. I was still undecided on what I wanted to become and unsure of what life was all about. All I knew then was that you needed money to survive. As a student, my social life also took up a lot of my time. When we partied we partied hard; we were irresponsible and silly.

- *3. Work ten times harder than the rest*

I grabbed every opportunity that came my way with both hands. I worked longer hours outside my normal working hours to develop myself in different departments. At the time my development started, I was still studying and everyone expected me to go into the fitness instructor/manager/ personal trainer direction. I didn't go that direction and neither did anyone force me into that direction. I was approached by the Administration Manager of the facility, who had seen the potential in me and asked me if I would be interested in becoming her assistant. I immediately said, 'Yes' and started my training in admin. I was in her office every day, asking questions and wanting to know more. She was strict and did everything in the right way. Admin was black on white; there was no in between or maybe. You either did it right or you would get a warning. People were scared of her so they did not make mistakes. Reception and sales departments made sure they did their jobs correctly. She was the best at what she did then and taught me about discipline and that you must stand your ground when you make a decision. There were many conflicts in the admin department, not between my manager and me, but between admin and the other departments. Admin is a dictator and a telling department; you tell people what to do and they must do it. The risk to the company is high; excuses do not make the risk less.

We worked well together in our administration team and what I most enjoyed was the structure that she taught me. Every hour there was something that needed to happen and there was a critical path that had to be followed every day for the department to be successful. For a person who does not like structure, admin can either make or break you.

- *4. It's not about the money, it's about the passion*

A few months later, I was promoted to Assistant Administrator, travelling between the two Gym branches in the city. During this time I bought myself a second hand car. She was a beautiful car for a student and was very fuel-efficient. I did not have enough money to pay my rent and for the car so my grandmother would give me money every month to help me out. Thanks to her, my life was made a little easier. When I bought the car, I promised my gran that I would get promoted and would soon be able to pay for my own car and rent.

The car that I had before was a 1.6 fuel injection model which I bought for R16 000 cash when I arrived back in South Africa after my working holiday in Europe. That car had a racing clutch, five gears and, I thought, electric windows. However, the electric windows only worked on good days. My car's life came to an end one day when it was parked in the parking area of the Mall. A lady driving a big truck reversed into my car's radiator with her big caravan tow bar, which went straight through the radiator. I didn't see it happen but when I got back to my car, it had a letter on it saying, 'I'm sorry,' together with her phone number. My car didn't make it to the end of the day. As I started it, it blew a head gasket. My dad organised a friend to fetch the car and take it straight to the dealer to sell. I sold it for more than I had bought it for, I still don't know how that happened.

After eight months of working as an Assistant Administrator, I was promoted again. My new title was Club Administrator so I became an Admin Manager. My pay increased to R5 000 and

I thought that this was it. With this money I could buy a house. And I did buy a townhouse; on that salary, the bank agreed to give me a loan as long as my dad signed surety.

It's now 10 years later and I'm still working for the Gym. The investments and decisions I made 10 years ago have had a massive impact on my living standard today. I have a passion and my purpose is to work for a great company.

- *5. Train, coach and mentor people to become better than you are*

As a very young Administration Manager, I needed a very strong leader and mentor to guide me. He was a special man who had passion and patience, although having both those values together is rare. He taught me structure, time management and, most importantly at that stage, how to make decisions. He always told me that when you are an Admin Manager, you cannot be popular because you have to make hard financial decisions in an area where the risk is high. I did not know much about being a manager, never mind about being a leader. He is one of the reasons why I am who I am today as he invested time in me. He allowed me to make mistakes, but never to make the same mistake twice. I can still remember that in one of my performance evaluations, I told him that I was not very innovative. I said that in admin I could not be innovative because there is only one way of doing things and that is the right way.

His response was a game-changer for me; he said that I had the potential to be innovative. I could come up with great business ideas in any department I worked in. The ideas did not have to be admin oriented, as long as they were better, more practical and potentially cost saving innovative ideas. You will be innovative when you challenge the norm daily and reward innovative thinking.

I looked at him questioningly, not knowing what to make of his response. But I know that I walked out of his office and started searching for innovation everywhere. I never stopped listening to the gurus as I was always looking for wisdom. *I can advise you that whenever you have a performance evaluation, try and remember the good things that were said. Don't be like the average person who will only remember the one bad thing that was said. Average people will not hear the 15 good things said about their performance, they will only remember the bad things. Focus on what you do well. Become so good at what you do well that people won't notice your weaknesses.*

It is also important to make yourself replaceable. When you get promoted, you are accountable to ensure there is someone able to do the job as well, or even better, than you did it, to take over from you. Companies will not promote people if they do not have a replacement for them. The responsibility for doing that training and development lies with you as the leading individual in whatever department you serve in.

Remember the importance of being kind and generous to everyone you deal with at work or in your personal life. Anyone can become your boss one day. You never know.

- *6. Uphold a great name and lead by example*

We would meet during the day and in the evenings our regional business support team would take us out for dinner. One night we went to a very fancy and expensive restaurant and all the important financial staff from head office also attended the dinner. I was not used to that type of food or the ambiance of that type of venue but I tried to fit in and look as if I knew what I was doing. It wasn't long before I realised that I wasn't the only one feeling out of place when I noticed a lady start waving her fork in the air, mashed potatoes flying all over the place. She spoke with her mouth full and people started starring at her. I realised that she was on her sixth double brandy and coke and when I tried to tell her to take it slowly, she started speaking louder. She pointed her fork at the people from head office who were sitting directly opposite us. The Brandy lady looked around the table with blood red eyes, she paused for a second and then her head dropped onto her plate. Face first into her mashed potatoes. It took us the rest of the evening to get her back to her guest house.

At breakfast the next morning, the lady sharing a room with her was pale. We asked her what had happened, she said that Brandy girl had climbed into the shower and while she was showering, she passed out and broke the shower partitioning. The water kept running and flooded the entire room. The lady sharing with her was still fairly new at that stage and she resigned a month after the incident. Brandy girl was eventually dismissed for stealing her own petty cash.

It can take you years to build a good name but you can lose that good name in one night, by sending one email or by having the wrong attitude.

- *7. Live each day as if it is payday*

As human beings, we spend money we don't have before we have it. I learnt that we go through every month wishing for payday to arrive. When payday does come, we are happy for one day and then we start wishing for payday again. It took me years to change my thinking around this principle but I eventually realised that if I kept on wishing for payday, I would get to the end of my life realising that life had gone by so quickly and all I had wished for was payday. Why didn't I live every day as if it was payday?

To be honest, it took me six years to change my thinking regarding money. When I got promoted to Admin Manager, I thought that my R5 000 salary was enough and that I now had a townhouse and a good car. I then got stuck in the same position for four years. I progressed through the ranks quickly at the beginning of my career because I wanted more. Achieving the title of Manager made me want less and my drive to become more disappeared. All I did every month was wish for payday. All I wanted was to pay my bills and to get it over with. I realised then that I would never be happy with my salary because every time I got promoted and got more money, at the end of the month I was still left with R50 in my bank account. I know I'm not the only one and I'm sure many people can identify with this situation.

It is amazing to see staff morale when people receive increases. They smile and are happy and it looks as if they now have enough money and can live comfortably. Three months down the line, the increase they got is no longer enough because we adjust our lifestyles even before we receive the increase. As human beings it is difficult for us to not adjust our lifestyles and increase our expenditure when we expect an increase. Often even before we have the money, we start living a more expensive life and the simple truth is that we will *never* have enough money.

My advice to you is to accept the fact and to stop wishing for payday to arrive. Start living life as if every day is payday. Show gratitude for what you have and stay humble.

When I look at my staff on payday, thirteen years down the line, I see the happiness on their faces. You see burgers, fried chicken and pizza when you walk into the kitchen. You hear laughter and see happy faces. For the first week of the month, it is happiness all around our work place. As the month progresses, you start seeing people eating two minute noodles and white bread with milk. You see cheaper meals like Russian sausage and chips or chicken livers with brown bread. The conversations in the kitchen are now about how they are wishing for payday again.

I started thinking about how I had longed for Fridays when I was at to boarding school. Just as I had then wished the week would pass, the staff is wishing for each month to pass more quickly, for payday to arrive.

Think about when you will be 80 years old. When you look back on your life, how do you want to remember it? Will you only remember how you wished for payday? We wish our lives away, we continually wish for Fridays and better days yet we do not make an effort to create a better life for ourselves.

Stop wishing for paydays and Friday and start living every day as if it is Friday. Leave a legacy so that people will remember you for living each day fully. With passion, love and energy.

Ask yourself the question: 'Is that a life that was worth living for?'

- *8. Become so great at what you do, that people can't stop talking about you*

After four years of being an admin manager, I met my ex. She was bright, funny and damn intelligent. She was busy doing her Master's degree in Microbiology and I was fascinated and inspired by how she went about her life striving to learn more every single day. I realised that I did not want to be average anymore so I made a choice to start being more passionate about my job and the fact that I wanted to move ahead. I applied for an Operations Manager position twice but was only appointed after my second application.

When I got the position, I was flattered and my focus and drive to be the best Operations Manager of the year was my driving force. I had to do most of my training, learning and development myself and when I did not know what to do, I made a plan to find out. I learnt how to repair a toilet seat. I learnt about pools, plant rooms, maintenance and health and safety; for the first time in four years I was actually working and enjoying it. At that time I had a General Manager who became a very good friend. We grew together through the ranks, he just moved faster than I did. He didn't get stuck, although he did leave the company for a while to go and work on cruise ships. He came back after three months, having realised that the grass is not greener on the other side of the wellness industry. I learnt from him that teaching people to think out of the box is the best type of learning. If you do not get something the first time it is said, you need to get the knowledge from elsewhere. At this learning stage of my life, I have also learnt that as a leader you need to make time for every single staff member. If you choose to develop only one person, you might miss another talented person. Structure and plan your time in order to make time for each individual. Every single person working with you has the ability to learn and to get more knowledge. It is up to you as a leader to know your people and to teach and mentor them in what they want to know.

If you see people grow and become better than you are, you know that you've done your job. Don't get left behind. Focus on what you want to be and then go for it.

It took me a little over a year to feel I was fantastic as an Operations Manager. I was happy with the results but felt empty and was yearning to learn more. I was not getting the stimulation that I wanted and I felt neglected. I also did not feel appreciated and didn't want to work for the company anymore. That was the first and last time that I have applied for positions outside the wellness industry. I didn't apply for other jobs because I wanted to, I applied because I was bored in my current position. I can still remember when I sent my CV to the company where I was applying for another job. As the fax was going through, a man walked into my office. The Regional Business Manager at that time and he wanted to tell me something. I went blood red because I thought that he had seen me faxing my CV but I was wrong. He had come to tell me that I had been nominated as one of the Top Five Operations Managers of the Year. I'd be going to the yearly awards ceremony where the announcement would be made of the Operations Manager of the year. I was excited and confused. I realised that they had seen my potential and had actually noticed the great work that I was doing. It was a great feeling. Aimee and I went shopping for an outfit for me to wear on the gala evening of The Star Awards. I decided to keep my outfit plain and simple but stylish and professional.

When the night finally arrived, I was nervous, scared, excited and did not know what to expect. When they announced our category the five finalists walked onto the stage. As I looked around me, I saw very talented and highly recommended Operations Managers. I got even more scared; my mouth was dry and my legs were shaking.

'And the winner is... – Serijke Grobler!' I can still remember the cheers and applause from the crowd, I remember each and every sound and face that I connected with while standing on the stage. I accepted my award. As I tried to walk, my legs felt like jelly but I could feel a smile on my face that was as big as a crevasse in the Grand Canyon. I've never been as proud of myself as I was on that day. I realised again that people see what you do when you work hard, when you make your work a priority and when you bring innovation to your work. They see how you adapt to change. People see when you want something more and when you want to learn more.

The importance of achieving exceptional results continuously and consistently plays a massive role in your career. Four years after winning the award as Top Operations manager, I was nominated and in the Top Five for the award as Top General Manager in the country.

- *9. Build relationships with mentors and leaders*

About three months after receiving the award, I applied for the General Manager position. The interview and appointment processes took a very long time and I can remember how tense and nervous I was while waiting to get the news. The business manager walked into my office again and said that my time had come. He also said that he could not appoint me as it would be up to the new Regional Business Manager, to make a decision on the appointment.
I was confused again as I did not know who the new person was and he also did not know who I was. How was I going to make an impression on him if I hadn't worked with him before? When I met him for the first time I did not know what to expect. Here was this big man standing in front of me and when I say big, I mean strong and with massive muscles. He asked me a few questions and immediately said that I had the job so I then became a General Manager. Many years of hard work and dedication had paid off!

I built a great relationship with him and a strong bond formed between us. I had and still have a great deal of respect for him and was devastated when he was promoted and left my region for another one. He guided and mentored me at the very beginning of my leadership days. We shared many jokes and he accepted me for who I am. He is a big man with an even bigger heart and he is a great mentor and leader.

I worked at the branch for two years and then wanted a new challenge as I felt my work at that branch was complete. I'd had to endure many facility refreshes and upgrades. Although I had a strong bond with the staff and members it was time for something fresh and new. I was promoted.

Since I had started at that club in 2001, it had always been my dream to lead the team as General Manager there. I had visualised myself in the General Manager's chair many years before I was appointed.

- *10. Lead without a title*

You can lead if you are a street-sweeper. You can lead if you pack the groceries in a supermarket. At the end of the day the street sweeper will get buried next to the president, the MD of a company will be buried next to the cleaner. On your gravestone there will be no title. You don't reserve the best and highest spot in the cemetery, every spot in the cemetery is equally important. That's why it is so important to lead by example and to treat everyone as equals.
Start being a leader where you are right now. Don't wait for a title. Work every day as if you are already a General Manager. Take responsibility for your life and your decisions. Don't wait for people to make decisions for you. Be accountable for your actions and for the decisions you make.

We employed a less fortunate guy who had grown up in a home for abandoned children as a cleaner. I saw potential in this guy and really wanted to see him excel. I was not surprised when I received feedback from members saying that he was amazing. On a quiet Sunday afternoon when there is not much to do or clean in the facility, he took a toothbrush and started cleaning the grout in the men's change room with it. He was on his knees, cleaning every little corner in the change room. He worked as if he was being supervised but no one was watching him or telling him what to do. He was passionate about cleaning; he was proud and grateful for his job. *He* leads without a title.

- *11. Never employ your best friend*

We spend most of our days at work, 80% of our lives is spent at work. The 20% we spend with our friends and family mainly happens on weekends. Most of the time when we work with great people, we tend to become friends. The question is, how do you balance the relationship and stay professional when you are friends? In my experience I have only had heartache and disappointment when it comes to working with friends, especially in the same facility, and the same goes for family.
We think we have it under control, that when you work with your best friend or family, they will never disappoint you. It is easier to trust them and when you trust people in business, you don't check on them regularly. You focus more on the people who are under-performing. As a leader, you then leave your best friend to do their own thing.

What I learnt was that when money is involved, people change. People will do anything to make money, even committing fraud, stealing and things they would never previously have done. Money makes people evil and it makes people do evil things.

When people are pushed to perform and to achieve results through other people, they will bring other people down with them. Leaders either build other people or they break them down. It was really hard for me to see how this happened under my leadership. I was blinded by my best friend and the day I realised what was happening, was the day it was too late. The damage had been done.

Sitting in a misconduct hearing and asking the chairperson for the harshest sanction is not easy. Dismissing my best friend was one of the hardest things I have had to do in my entire career. What he did and the decisions he made almost ruined my 15 year career as a General Manager.

What we as a heads of department team had worked on for two years, his decisions and what he allowed his team to do almost destroyed us. It cost us dearly and we dropped in performance in only one day.

I had to add this bonus point to this chapter. *The day that you think you know or when you think you have seen everything, is the day you should get worried. Always be on guard, what you think is happening is not always the thing that is happening. Trust your gut feeling. You cannot trust anyone where money is involved. Not your family and not your best friend...*

Chapter Seventeen

Overcoming Daily Challenges

So has it been easy to achieve success in my career despite my disability? And does the fact that I am physically different to other people bother me? Yes, I am self-conscious, shy and I do get angry when people stare at the way I walk. My feet slap on the floor when I walk and the loud noise that echoes as I walk along is highly frustrating and annoying. When I walk in a mall or at work, I pass many people; some whom I know, others whom I don't. Some people will recognise me although I don't know them. When people stare at the way I walk, their mouths fall open. It is almost as if I can see the way their faces change, they go into this mode of thinking, 'I wonder what happened to her?'

They will be so focused on my funny walk that they won't see my smile, friendly eyes or the cheerful expression on my face. They will not notice me greeting them. Some people will even gossip and laugh at me. It makes me remember how I was teased and stepped on at a younger age. People will talk down to me and will speak negatively about me behind my back, even though they don't know me.

As I walk around the gym to do quality checks, greeting members and assisting on the gym floor, members talk to me all the time. They give me either good or bad feedback. At the beginning of my career, it was hardly possible for me to walk the floor. Members would walk up to me and ask if I had been in an accident or have a prosthetic leg. When you tell them that you have muscular dystrophy, most people ask what that is. Spending time explaining the condition to people just gets to be too much effort. Imagine seeing about 1 500 members a day; you would end up speaking to about 50 members per day! How would I stay positive and do what I am paid to do if I had to do that?

My tips on how to stay positive in challenging times, when you are faced with a disease or chronic illness:

- When you wake up in the morning, think of five things that you are *grateful* for. How you adore your family, how grateful you are for your friends and how you are an encourager to every person who crosses your path.

- Instead of asking God to take your disease or disability away, thank Him for making you the way you are. There is always something to be *thankful* for. Say thank you, instead of asking for something. Honour your talents, express your gifts and reveal your creativity to everyone around you.

- *Mind feeding* for at least 15 minutes in the mornings. Get up and do your reading, read anything that motivates or inspires you. It could be a TED talk, business reading or just an inspirational story. Learn something new every day. Nourish your soul.

- *Exercise is medicine.* Get up and get active. Daily exercise will decrease your pain. It will give you energy and help you to focus. You need to cherish your health.

- *Healthy eating* and controlling your weight. There is no quick fix, diet or pill that will control your weight for you. You are in control of what you put into your mouth. Enjoy what you eat, do not make food your enemy. If you overeat and over-drink, you will gain weight and become unhealthy. Eat and drink in moderation. Keep a balance in everything.

- *Positive affirmations* are a powerful game changer. Stand in front of a mirror and tell yourself at least five times how awesome you are. You can use your own affirmations. Know that you are strong and brave, not timid or weak. Every day in every way I become better and better.

- Set *five little goals* on a daily basis. Reflect on your goals and read them every day. By the end of every week you will have achieved 35 small goals. By the end of the month, you should have achieved 1 050 goals. Breaking your goals down into smaller, daily goals will give you a boost. You will be able to celebrate each daily goal that you have achieved. Be wise and know that your past will no longer limit your future. Just because you didn't achieve something yesterday, doesn't mean you aren't able to achieve it today.

- Set a *high standard* for yourself. Get up in the mornings, get dressed and be proud of who you are. Chin up and chest out. Stay loyal to your values, be respectful of your mission and fiercely focused on becoming your dreams.

- *Visualisation and positive thinking* – when you have a tough day, reflect on why you are doing what you are doing for a living. Or on why you are here on earth. Never become the victim of anyone's words or deeds. Be the giver, not the taker.

- When you *fall,* you will fall hard. Stand up, learn from your mistakes and strive to become an icon in your work. Never doubt yourself or your abilities. You might walk funny or have a limp or deformity. Accept it. Your mind is the strongest organ in your body. Use it wisely.

- You become the person that you surround yourself with. If you surround yourself with people who say you can't do it, you will not be able to do it. If you surround yourself with positive thinkers and go-getters, you will become a go getter. Surround yourself with people who are smarter, faster, stronger and better than you are. People who will lift you with their morals and inspire you by their example.

- The only thing you cannot buy is *time*. Use every minute in your day to be productive. Plan your day properly and allocate times to ever task that needs to be done. Learn to say 'no' to time wasters. Prioritise your day into urgent and important. You will always have time for tasks, if you make time for them.

- Things will not always go according to plan. Be part of the *solution* and never be part of the problem.

- You have to *be different* to make a difference. Your disease or illness will make or break you. You can either become your disease or you can take charge of it and be more than just your condition. Live the life that you want to live, there is a reason why you are different. Use it to your advantage. Inspire people with your actions.

- It is important to *laugh* a lot, to laugh until your stomach aches. *Love* with your whole heart. *Celebrate* every win in life and at work. *Believe* and know that you are the leader of your faith, the owner of the results you achieve and the hero of your own destiny.

To all the readers of my book I say, understand that there is no miracle, special treatment or cure for many diseases. Believe and invest in what you can control, which is your thinking and your mind set. You are in charge of your thinking. You are in charge of your choices. Take accountability, accept who you are and live life according to your normal. Live beyond what others see as your limits.

Chapter Eighteen

The Midnight Wake-up Call

I'm awake! It is one o'clock in the morning. Sweat is running down my back. I have this pain in my chest creating a very uncomfortable feeling. Is this an anxiety attack?

I can't breathe, I'm gasping for air, and I'm confused beyond thinking. Am I awake? Or is this a horrible dream? I'm slapping myself in the face, trying to wake up. I start screaming, 'Wake-up Siekie, wake-up!'

This is just a nightmare. This is only a dream. This can't be real. Or is it real?

As I started to realise that it was not a dream, it was reality, I thought to myself, 'How on earth did I get to this point in my life?'

After eight years of building a relationship, working through difficult times and building a life together, the reality had set in - this relationship was over...

It was a normal month end Saturday for me. Early morning and I was ready for work as January in the fitness industry means long hours and very busy days. I knew that I had not spent a lot of time at home that January. It was work, work and more work. When I got home in the evenings, I was tired, not in the mood to talk. I just sat and stared at the television.

That specific Saturday was different. It was the Saturday that brought an end to an exciting phase of my life and the start of a new chapter. I came home after a long morning and as usual, I went and lay on our bed to have an afternoon nap. For the first time in many years, Aimee was not home. She was always home when I got back from work. She had told me that morning that she was going to the art gallery with one of our best friends. She said she had to speak to the friend urgently about the matter which I had discussed with her a month before. The matter in question was that Aimee was spending too much time with our best friend and I thought that they were becoming too close. In my experience with gay women, friends and relationships, when you get too much attention from your best friend, you need to set boundaries. It is a proven fact that most gay women fall in love with their best friends.

I am an example of this fact as I fell in love with my best friend after sharing a boarding school room with her for three years. We did not touch each other or declare that we were gay during our school years and then both went overseas for a year after finishing school. She went to America and I went to Europe. When we got back we shared a student house, becoming roommates again. We no longer had the pressure of school and we could become what we really are. Our relationship went from being best friends to lovers. When we first kissed, we both felt the same way. Knowing that best friends can fall in love, I now suspected something between Aimee and our best friend.

When Aimee got home, she came and lay next to me on our bed. I asked her if everything was in order as she looked very worried. She looked into my eyes and told me that there was sexual tension between her and our best friend. She then asked how I felt about her and our relationship. I responded by telling her that I loved her and that she still gave me butterflies in my stomach when I looked at her. She replied, 'I don't feel the same. To me our relationship feels as if we are best friends.'

I could feel how my heart was being ripped from my chest. I had to go to the toilet, my stomach started running and I thought about incidents that I've handled in the gym before. Just before people have a heart attack, their stomachs often start to run. 'Am I having a heart attack?' I thought.

I started crying, screaming and feeling like a lost person. Was this really happening to me again?

She said that what we had was everything she had ever wanted in a relationship and in life. She said that she loved me so much and that she did not want to hurt me. She needed time to think, I needed to give her a month to think about what she wanted. She wanted to move into the spare room. I did not know what to say or think; to me the entire situation felt unreal. 'I've given her everything I could possibly give. I've changed who I am for her; I've created a life that she wanted. I made her happy. I bought her presents she wanted. I've given her love. Where did I go wrong? Or should I rather ask, were did we go wrong?' Thoughts like these raced through my mind.

The saying goes, 'When one door closes, another always opens, there is an opportunity behind the new door.' It is up to you what you attract in life. If you choose to be happy, happiness will come to you. This was the affirmation I had written on a piece of paper that I'd put next to my bed. I read it every morning to get myself going for the new day. It was now really hard to get myself out of bed.

Financially I was back to square one. A break-up is never easy and the things that you and your partner bought together have to be split between you. I had to take over the payments on the pick-up truck that we had bought together just six months prior to the break-up. I couldn't afford both my car and the pick-up truck and it was necessary for me to take action and control over my life. The car dealership that assisted me was really helpful and helped me to get a good trade in on both vehicles. The only car that the dealership could give me at a price that I could afford, was a Red family car. It was not ideal for me to drive a family car because I was single and on my own.

Little did I know that the red car would be the beginning of a new life. It marked a change and assisted me in setting new goals. My parents asked me why I had bought a family car. My response was simple, 'I will have a family and a baby seat on the back seat of my car before the end of this year.'

That would be a big statement for anyone to make. You cannot just create a family out of nothing and being gay does not make it any easier. Most people thought it was a joke when I told them my dream but I knew that I would achieve my goal, as long as I believed that it was possible. I'd seen many miracles in my life and believed I could witness more.

One Sunday morning after my two best friend's wedding, I woke up. At the wedding a friend had asked me if I was ready for a relationship again. My response was, 'Yes I am ready. I want to flirt with someone.' I got the number and name of a girl who had just returned from the UK and was single and looking for love. Like everybody always does, I went onto social media to check out the unknown person. I saw a very beautiful woman with a beautiful two year-old boy. As I went through her profile, I felt a tingling in my stomach. A gut feeling; butterflies are an understatement. This woman was what I wanted. She had blonde hair and a sexy body. It took me an hour to get the message that I wanted to send to her perfect. I knew that first impressions always last so I wanted to make the right one.

Three days after the first message, she invited me for coffee at her house to meet her and her little boy. Little did I know that I would meet practically her entire family that night too. I have never drunk so much coffee in my life. The only thing I wanted to do was to kiss this women sitting in front of me. I did not hear a word that the people said around me, I was completely focused on her. It was love at first sight. When I saw her, I knew that we would be together. I had to wait for the family to leave and I then gave a big sigh and asked her for a glass of wine. We sat down and talked for a while. Again, I did not hear a word she was saying. All I heard and saw were her lips, her soft skin and her beautiful dimples at the sides of her mouth.

Politely I asked her if I could hold her hand. As I took her hand in mine, I could see her becoming more relaxed. As she was telling me about something, I told her to pause her story. 'I'm going to kiss you now,' I said. She did not have time to say anything back. That was the start of our new relationship. Not only the start of a new life for me, but also a new life for her. I told her after kissing for a long time that I was hungry. She got up and made me a sandwich with Bovril on it. I told her that the sandwich she'd made was my favorite. We knew instantly that we were meant to be.

She had been married to her husband for six years. At the time we started seeing each other, they were going through a divorce. She told me that she had tried for many years to be straight, to be the person the world wanted her to be. The normal that the world created for her was that she had to be straight. She conformed to the world's belief and she did love her husband very much. He is a great guy and looked after them well. What she couldn't take any longer was that she had a burning desire to be with a woman. She first fell in love with her best friend but the friend was not interested in a relationship with her. She and her husband decided to move back to South Africa to try and see if their relationship could still work. The desire to be with a woman did not go away and she decided to see a psychiatrist. The psychiatrist told her that she should move on with her life and get a divorce. She went to a psychiatric hospital for two weeks and was given anti-depressants.

After our first night, she told me that the next day she had ended the casual relationship she had with another lady. I was very impressed with myself. After just four days of knowing her, I gave her the key to my house. She was very impressed with herself at achieving that in just four days. We were not complete strangers as we had gone to the same school. I was in grade 12 when she was in grade 8 and she knew exactly who I was. She knew that I had a disease and could remember the day I received a special award for great sportsmanship and perseverance at school. That was at the last prize giving of my school career.

I also remembered her as being a great swimmer.

I had my new red car, my beautiful blonde woman and a very handsome boy. I just knew that we would be together. You can never promise to be with someone forever as there are no guarantees in life. ***The advice I can give is to love the person you have every day, as if it is forever. There is no point in life to wish for better days. You need to do the work, to visualise better things for yourself. For you to attract what you want.***

You will feel and see if someone really is falling in love with you. Look and stare deeply into their eyes. Listen with intent; see what they are thinking through their eyes. Be mindful when you get to know the person. You will see and feel how much the person adores you. Feel it, look for it and you will see and find it. The deeper you stare into their eyes, the more uncomfortable they will become. That is when you will see a sign of fear. You can choose to live towards their fear or away from it. If you move away from the fear, you may just have missed the love of your life.

Say I love you first, be who you want to be, work like there is no tomorrow.

That is life; it starts with you.......

Glossary of Terms and Abbreviations

TERM	LANGUAGE	ENGLISH MEANING
AED	English	Automatic External Defibrillator
Airwolf	English	An American television series that ran from 1984 until 1987. The program centres on a high-tech military helicopter, code named *Airwolf*, and its' crew as they undertake various missions, many involving espionage, with a Cold War theme.
Aromat	English	Aromat is the brand name of a mass-produced general-purpose seasoning produced in Switzerland and South Africa under the brand name Knorr, which is owned by the Unilever group.
Biltong	Afrikaans	Lean meat that is salted and dried in strips.
Braai	Afrikaans	Barbeque
Brakenjan	Afrikaans	Afrikaans children's programme with a dog as the hero.
CMT1	English	Charcot Marie Tooth disease
Droewors	Afrikaans	A South African snack food, based on the traditional, coriander-seed spiced boerewors sausage
EMG	English abbreviation	Electromyography -is an electrodiagnostic medicine technique for evaluating and recording the electrical activity produced by skeletal muscles. EMG is performed using an instrument called an electromyograph, to produce a record called an electromyogram.
Haas Das	Afrikaans	Haas Das se Nuuskas was a weekly short television show in South Africa about a rabbit and a mouse running a news broadcast in Diere Land.
kaiings	Afrikaans	Crackling
Kanon	Afrikaans	Cannon

Knight Rider	English	An American television series created and produced by Glen A. Larson. The series was originally broadcast on NBC from 1982 to 1986. The show stars David Hasselhoff as Michael Knight, a high-tech modern crime fighter assisted by KITT, an advanced artificially intelligent, self-aware and nearly indestructible car.
Krummelpap	Afrikaans	Crumbly maize porridge
Load shedding	English	Load shedding, or load reduction, is done countrywide in South Africa when necessary as a controlled option to protect the electricity system, When there is too much demand and too little supply, bringing the power system into an imbalance – tripping the Power system in its entirety.
MacGyver	English	An American action-adventure television series created by Lee David Zlotoff. Henry Winkler and John Rich were the executive producers. The show ran for seven seasons on ABC in the United States and various other networks abroad from 1985 to 1992.
MD	English abbreviation	Managing Director
MD	English abbreviation	Muscular dystrophy is a group of diseases that cause progressive weakness and loss of muscle mass. In muscular dystrophy, abnormal genes (mutations) interfere with the production of proteins needed to form healthy muscle.
Nommer Asseblief	Afrikaans	Number please - this was a comedic South African television programme in the late '70s/early 80s.
Onze Rust	Afrikaans	Our Rest - name of President Steyn's farm
Phuza	Zulu	A Zulu word meaning 'drink'
Plankie	Afrikaans	Board, small wooden plank
President M.T. Steyn	English	Lawyer, prosecutor, State President of the OFS 1896-1902
Rooikat	Afrikaans	Caracal
Sot	Afrikaans	fool; foolish; mad; nonsensical

Tabasco sauce	English	A pungent sauce made from the fruit of a capsicum pepper.
Tuck	English	Snacks/food
Vetkoek	Afrikaans	Literally 'fat cake'. A traditional South African fried dough bread common in Afrikaner cookery. It is either served filled with cooked mince (ground beef) or with syrup, honey, or jam. It is thought to have its origins from the Dutch oliebollen.
Gym	English	An international group of gyms and health clubs
Wielie Walie	Afrikaans	Was an Afrikaans children's variety programme created by Louise Smit featuring puppets, which was broadcast from the launch of television in South Africa in 1976. With Karel and Sarel, two best friends but always fighting